Prehistory of the Southern Manabí Coast, Ecuador. López Viejo

Elizabeth J. Currie

BAR International Series 618
1995

Published in 2019 by
BAR Publishing, Oxford

BAR International Series 618

Prehistory of the Southern Manabí Coast, Ecuador. López Viejo

ISBN 9780860547990 paperback
ISBN 9781407349237 e-book

DOI https://doi.org/10.30861/9780860547990

A catalogue record for this book is available from the British Library

This book is available at www.barpublishing.com

BAR Publishing is the trading name of British Archaeological Reports (Oxford) Ltd. British Archaeological Reports was first incorporated in 1974 to publish the BAR Series, International and British. In 1992 Hadrian Books Ltd became part of the BAR group. This volume was originally published by Tempvs Reparatvm in conjunction with British Archaeological Reports (Oxford) Ltd / Hadrian Books Ltd, the Series principal publisher, in 1995. This present volume is published by BAR Publishing, 2019.

BAR titles are available from:

BAR Publishing
122 Banbury Rd, Oxford, OX2 7BP, UK
EMAIL info@barpublishing.com
PHONE +44 (0)1865 310431
FAX +44 (0)1865 316916
www.barpublishing.com

This report is dedicated to the memory of the late **Presley Norton Yoder**, founder of the Programa de Antropología para el Ecuador, who recommended this area of work to me during a visit to Ecuador in September 1991. Presley offered both moral and logistic support during the course of the fieldwork, and would have dearly loved to see this final product and the potential future work generated by our findings. It is greatly to be regretted that his death in Quito, on 8th May, 1993 meant that he never saw the end of the excavations at the Midden site.

CONTENTS

ACKNOWLEDGMENTS

I should like to take this opportunity to thank the following organisations and individuals for their contributions to this project.

The project was financed principally by a fellowship grant from the Leverhulme Trust and by additional funding from The Society of Antiquaries of London, without which, the work could never have been undertaken, and I am most grateful to both for their invaluable support.

Many individuals have contributed in large or small part to the successful running of the project, and of these, my thanks go foremost to my friend and colleague Kate Clark and to my husband Mark Steel. I thank Kate both for her work on the identification of the molluscan fauna, for many useful insights on the work generally, and for much invaluable advice and assistance with the computing, and I thank Mark for his moral support and for his bearing much of the overall responsibility for the running of the Trench A excavations. During the course of the excavations, I also owe thanks to the hard work and diligence of the Trench B supervisor Freddy Acuña who also bore much of the responsibility for the daily running of this unit, and, on occasion, Trench A. At the Centro de Investigaciones, Salango where the project was based, I should like to thank Patrick Gay who contributed much valuable work on the identification of the very considerable quantity of vertebrate remains.

In addition to Presley, another tragic and untimely death has been that of Carmen Lucas, in June 1994. Carmen oversaw much of the project post–excavation work and provided administrative assistance. I regarded her as a good friend and she will be much missed.

Eric López assisted me during the course of the Phase 1 Topographic Survey and finally I should thank Gerardo Castro in anticipation of his report on the lithics material.

York Survey Supply Centre provided the project with a range of survey equipment at cost price, for which I thank them.

Last, but certainly not least, I reserve a special place of continuing thanks to a dear friend Olaf Holm. From his position as Director of the Museo Antropológico, Guayaquil, Olaf has played a key role in the furtherance of Ecuadorean archaeological interests and provided support and encouragement to foreign researchers such as myself, over the course of many years.

CHAPTER 1

RECONNAISSANCE, SURVEY AND THE PHASES

AREA RECONNAISSANCE AND TOPOGRAPHIC SURVEY

Introduction

Following my original proposal for research funding to the Leverhulme Trust and to the Society of Antiquaries of London, the first stage of my planned programme of research involved the area reconnaissance and topographic survey of the eastern sector of the modern fishing town of Puerto López, Canton Jipijapa, southern Manabí province, Ecuador (Map 1), to identify the geographic spread of the original prehistoric settlement of this area.

Return to the site in October 1992 confirmed my earlier observations of the area made in 1991, that the encroachment of modern buildings eastward from the main town threatened the principal locus of prehistoric occupation in this area. Extensive surface scatters of prehistoric cultural material: principally pottery, large quantities of both worked stone and stone debitage and different species of marine shells and worked shell debitage, together with the remains of stone foundation walls outlining large domestic structures, attested to the density of the prehistoric occupation here. Several hectares of previously undeveloped land on the eastern boundary of modern Puerto López were found to be divided into small lots, already sold to different owners for building in the coming year (1993).

The Topographic Survey

During the first phase of the work, an area reconnaissance, surface collection and photographic record was made of the eastern sector of Puerto López (Map 2), in order to establish the principal locations of the ancient settlement here. An arbitrary site grid was laid out N – S/ E – W, to facilitate a detailed topographic contour survey of the area along the present–day eastern boundary of Puerto López, where the greatest concentrations of surface prehistoric cultural remains are found.

In the concluding stages of Phase One, a detailed contour map of one important area occupied during prehistory was produced (hereafter called "The South–Western Loma", being located on a low spur of land overlooking the modern town, and the most south– westerly extent of the ancient locus of settlement here). The contour map also includes the outlines of any structural walls located on the surface during the course of the survey (Map 3).

RESULTS AND CONCLUSIONS OF PHASE ONE

Locus of Ancient Settlement

The prehistoric occupation of López Viejo ("Old López") is located in different areas of the town, depending on the period and culture concerned. Successive "El Niño" rains through time, since the earliest occupation of this area, have resulted in high erosional effect and also deep alluvial depositions, separating the different occupations with many metres of sterile hill wash. Deep erosion gullies – "quebradas" – cut the land in places, affording useful "previews" of the cultural sequence in the profiles they create. These quebrada profiles were mapped and photographed wherever necessary, to assist in the process of recording the spread of prehistoric occupation across the town.

THE FORMATIVE PERIOD (ca 3500 BC – 300 BC)

Valdivia Culture

The earliest recorded occupation of López Viejo pertains to the Early Formative period Valdivia culture (ca 3500 BC – 1500 BC), and is located both in the surrounding low foothills (ca 100 metres above sea level) to the extreme east of the town, away from the coast, and also along the banks of a fossil river estuary, close to the sea. No evidence of Valdivia cultural material was found in surface collections made during the course of the Phase One reconnaissance and survey.

Machalilla Culture

Pottery dating to the succeeding Early Formative period Machalilla culture (ca 1500 BC – 1300 BC) is found both inside the perimeters of the modern town centre, close to the existing shoreline, and also higher up on what is now the modern–day cemetery, towards the back eastern edge of the town, upon a low spur of land. However, no Machalilla pottery was found in surface collections made during the course of the Phase One reconnaissance and survey.

Engoroy Culture

Late Formative period Engoroy pottery (ca 1200 BC – 300 BC) dominates the surface ceramic findings on the present eastern boundaries of the modern town, in the area most immediately threatened by building development. From the extent and amount of the surface findings of pottery dateable to this period, the Engoroy occupation was much larger than the earlier settlements of the Valdivia and Machalilla periods, and is associated with a worked stone industry (principally of local chert) of demonstrable importance. This can be related to the increasing importance of shell–working along this coast, where various species of marine shells: the red–rimmed *Spondylus princeps* and *Spondylus calcifer*, and the pearl oysters *Pteria sterna* and *Pinctada mazatlanica*, were exploited to manufacture fine shell artifacts for both

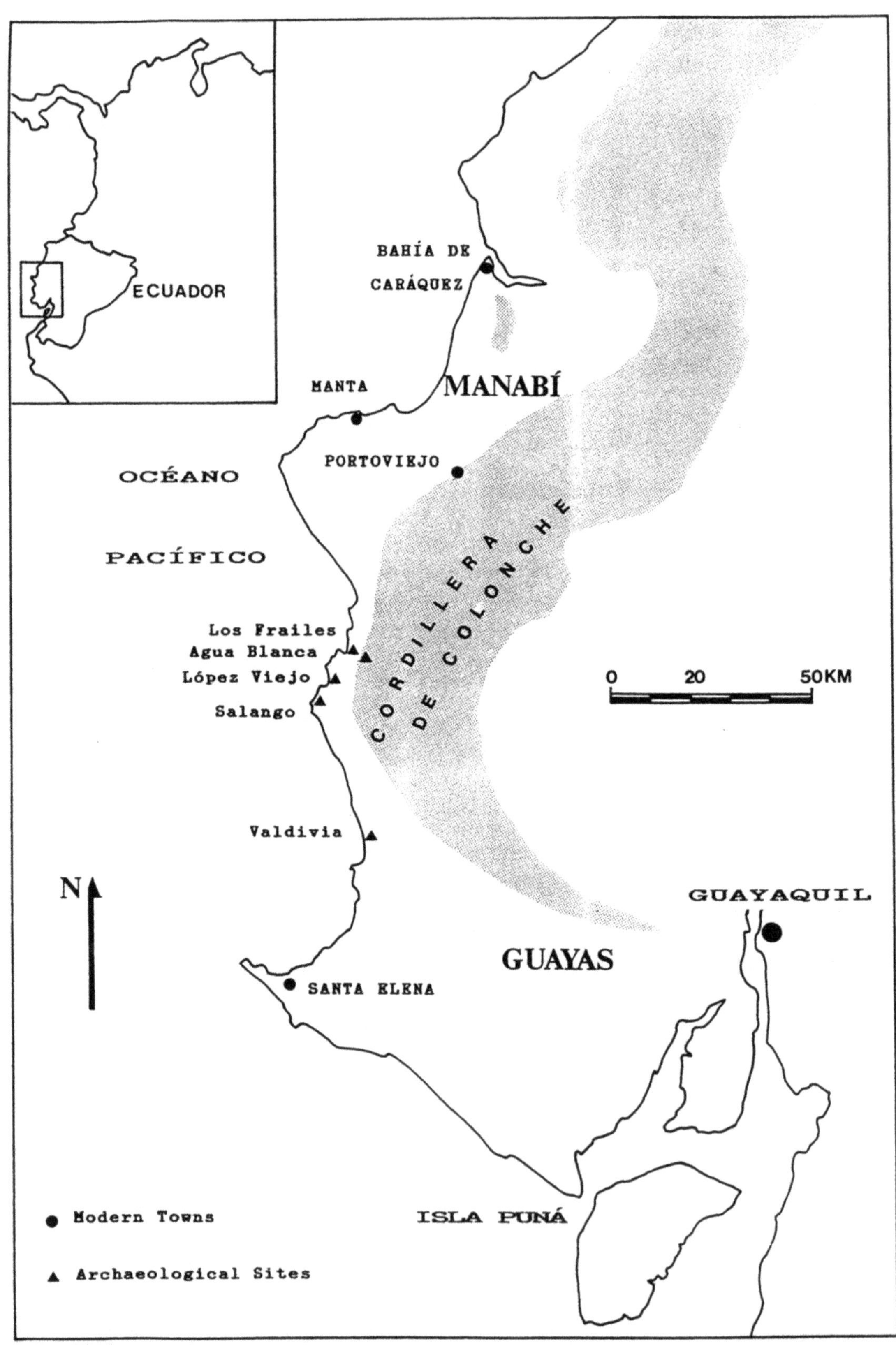

MAP1: SOUTH-CENTRAL COAST OF ECUADOR

local sumptuary use and long–distance trade.

REGIONAL DEVELOPMENTAL PERIOD (ca 300 BC – AD 800)

Bahía and Guangala Cultures

No certain evidence of Regional Developmental Period Bahía or Guangala cultures was found during the Phase One reconnaissance and survey, although earlier archaeological research in the general locality reports finding evidence of a dispersed settlement pattern of small–scale Guangala farmsteads on the surrounding hills. Both Bahía and Guangala culture pottery has been found during the course of excavations conducted in the fishing town of Salango, five kilometres to the south of Puerto López during the 1980s.

INTEGRATION PERIOD (ca AD 800 – AD 1532)

Manteño Culture

The latest prehistoric occupation of this region belongs to the Integration period Manteño culture. Many of the remaining visible stone foundation walls of large structures are believed to date to this period, and were subject to a survey in 1979 which showed a sizeable settlement of around a hundred building remains. Regrettably no fixed modern reference point was included on the drawn plan so it has proved impossible to locate individual structures with any confidence, or other features, such as the Midden site itself with relation to these. The main locus of Manteño settlement appears to be in the northern and north–east suburbs and boundaries of modern Puerto López, extending into the region of the "South–Western Loma" mapped during Phase One. Manteño pottery occurs in moderate quantities from surface contexts in these areas.

CHAPTER 2

THE ARCHAEOLOGICAL EXCAVATIONS

Introduction

Upon the conclusion of Phase One, the succeeding Phase Two of this study was regrettably delayed by three weeks, owing to problems obtaining excavation permits from the local small– holding owners. Attempts had been made to locate the owners during the course of Phase One, but this was hampered, firstly by the large number of different owners of the various small plots of land, by the fact that the majority of them lived in towns and villages at some distance from Puerto López and by the fact that until the conclusion of the reconnaissance and survey phase, it was not known exactly which areas were to be selected for a detailed archaeological study through excavation.

Two locations were originally selected for further investigation, based upon the results of the Phase One survey: the Midden Site and the Quebrada Site. However, following the first weeks of excavation at the Midden Site, and the quantity and concentration of special artifacts, pottery and faunal remains being recovered, it was decided that this area was of such potential value and importance as to justify a change of strategy by opening a second trench to the south of the first, and to abandon the original plan to test the Quebrada site until a later date.

The Midden Site (3 – 6N/71–76E of 1992/3 Site Survey Grid)
(Maps 2 and 3)

Location of the Midden Site is in the eastern sector of Puerto López, in the barrio called Míramar, on the southern side of the Avenida Ocho, opposite Casa #173 Familia Avila Pincay. The whole area is situated on the first low spur of land overlooking the town and the bay, at an altitude of around 20 metres.

Triangulation was carried out setting up the level over the 0N/75E grid peg, close to the south east corner of Trench A, and set to 0° North. A reading of 287° was then taken on the tip of the church spire in the centre of Puerto López, and then 28° on the lamppost #19 outside the lamppost of the Familia Avila Pincay house.

A prominent artificial mound of occupation material to the west of a Manteño period structure here had been selected as the first area for investigation, based upon its possible relationship with the structure, and by the fact that surface collections conducted here in the past had yielded an unusually large amount of worked chert, stone and worked shell, as well as pottery dating to both the Engoroy and Manteño periods. It was hoped that a connecting sequence between the two periods might be established here, together with evidence of the local lithic and shell–working industries.

Commencement of Excavation

Señor Tito Guitierez, the owner of the land plot (*terreno*) in the Míramar sector of Puerto López, where the Midden Site is located, was eventually located and, following arduous bargaining, permission for excavation given. The local people are prejudiced against foreign investigators here, and believe they will be robbed of valuable artifacts. A long and difficult process of diplomatic negotiation is necessary to educate people on the scientific value of studies such as these, which have been authorised by the Instituto Nacional de Patrimonio Cultural. Permission was eventually given to excavate a relatively small trench – 3 metres by 5 metres.

The entire surrounding area of the Midden Site was surveyed, with a series of spot–heights taken to create a more detailed contour plan of the site (Figure 1). In the first instance, a 3 x 5 metre trench was laid out, to cut an approximate quadrant through the mound of archaeological deposits here, co–ordinates conforming to the grid which had been established during Phase One, and extended at the beginning of Phase Two. Later, a second 3 x 3 metre unit (Trench B) was placed some 15 metres to the south of Trench A into the centre of a second low midden mound.

Excavation of Trench A commenced shortly before Christmas, continued until 26th May, 1993 and was supervised by English archaeologist Mark Steel. Excavation of Trench B commenced 24th February 1993, was concluded on 19th May 1993, and was supervised by Ecuadorian archaeologist Freddy Acuña. The author carried the overall responsibility and directorship of both these sites.

Excavation Methodology

Wherever possible, excavation was by stratigraphic contexts, and recording followed the single context planning system set out in The Museum of London Archaeological Site Manual (Spence, 1990), using the Harris Matrix (Harris, 1989). Until true stratigraphic contexts were encountered, excavated material was located within metre square sub–units, and within arbitrary contexts, measured by level. Munsell Soil Colour values and descriptions have been used to describe the colour of the archaeological sediments whilst damp. However, some of the final contexts excavated towards the end of the fieldwork were excavated dry, and this is indicated in parenthesis where appropriate.

Excavation of the archaeological contexts of both Trench A and B was carried out with trowel and fine instruments of excavation (eg plasterer's leaf), for the duration of most of the excavations. Towards the end, it was felt that the pressure of time and the encountering of heavy clay and gravel deposits justified the occasional use of mattocks.

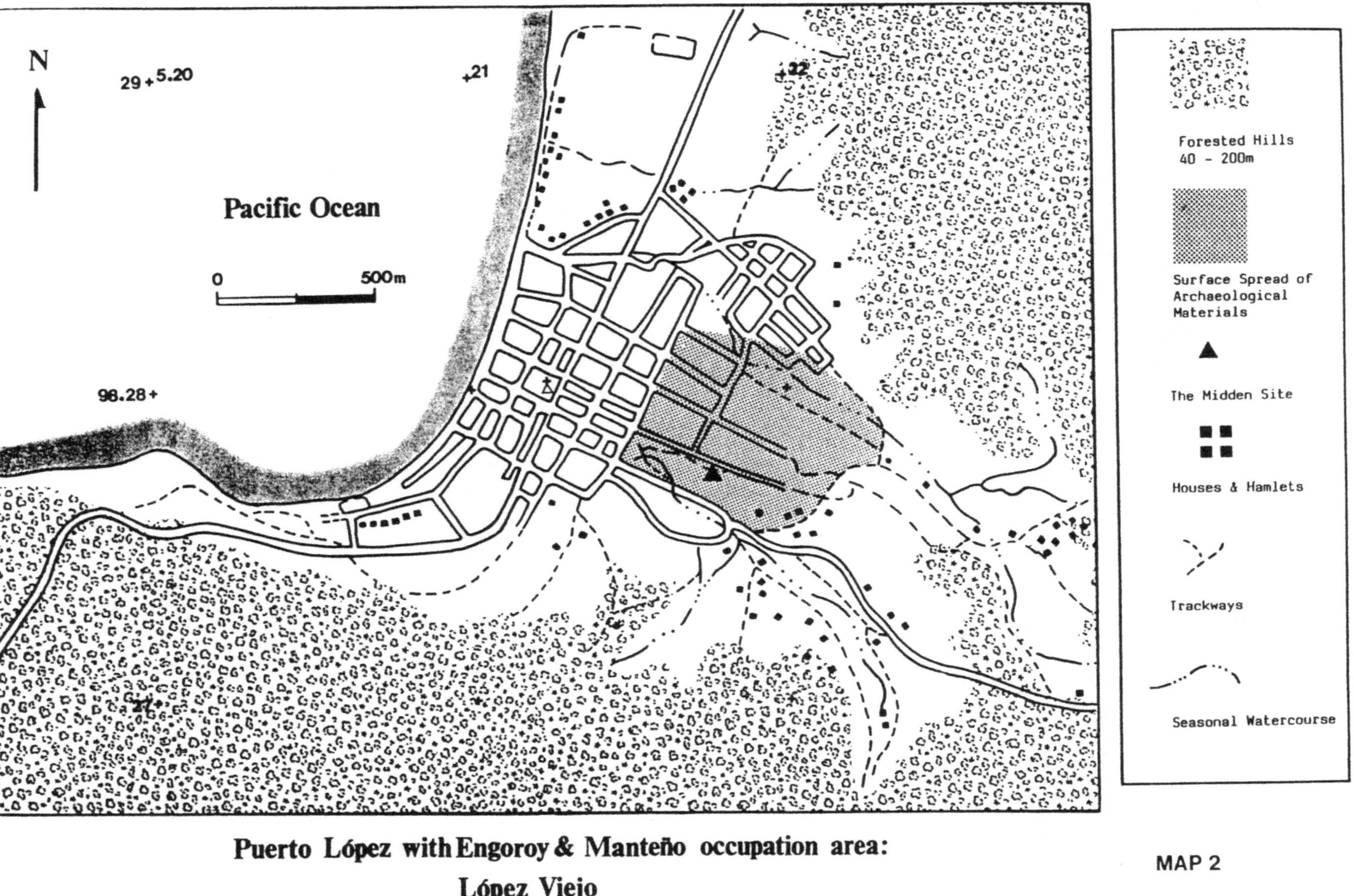

Puerto López with Engoroy & Manteño occupation area:
López Viejo

MAP 2

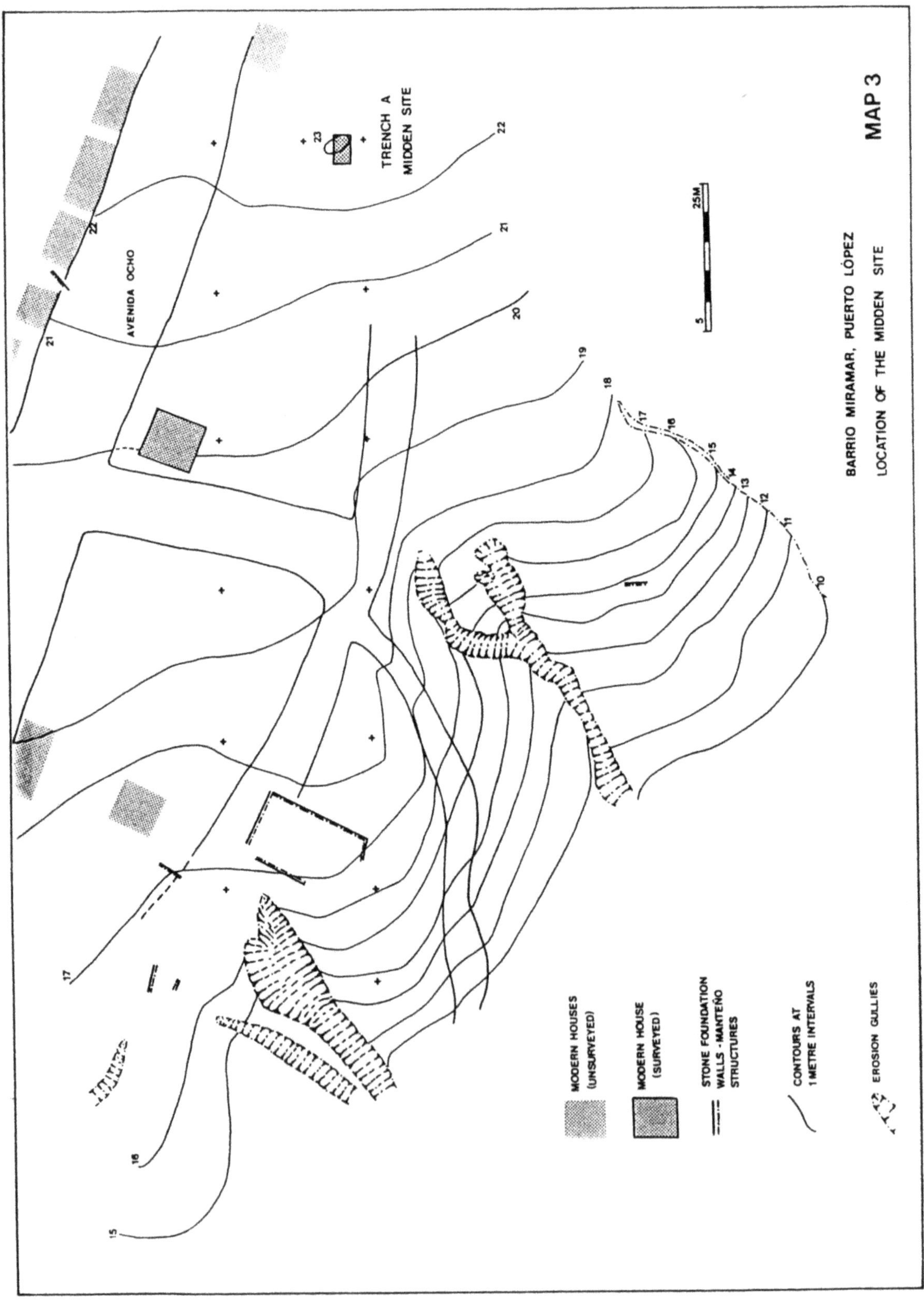
MAP 3
BARRIO MIRAMAR, PUERTO LÓPEZ
LOCATION OF THE MIDDEN SITE
TRENCH A
MIDDEN SITE
AVENIDA OCHO
5
25M
MODERN HOUSES (UNSURVEYED)
MODERN HOUSE (SURVEYED)
STONE FOUNDATION WALLS - MANTEÑO STRUCTURES
CONTOURS AT 1 METRE INTERVALS
EROSION GULLIES

FIGURE 1

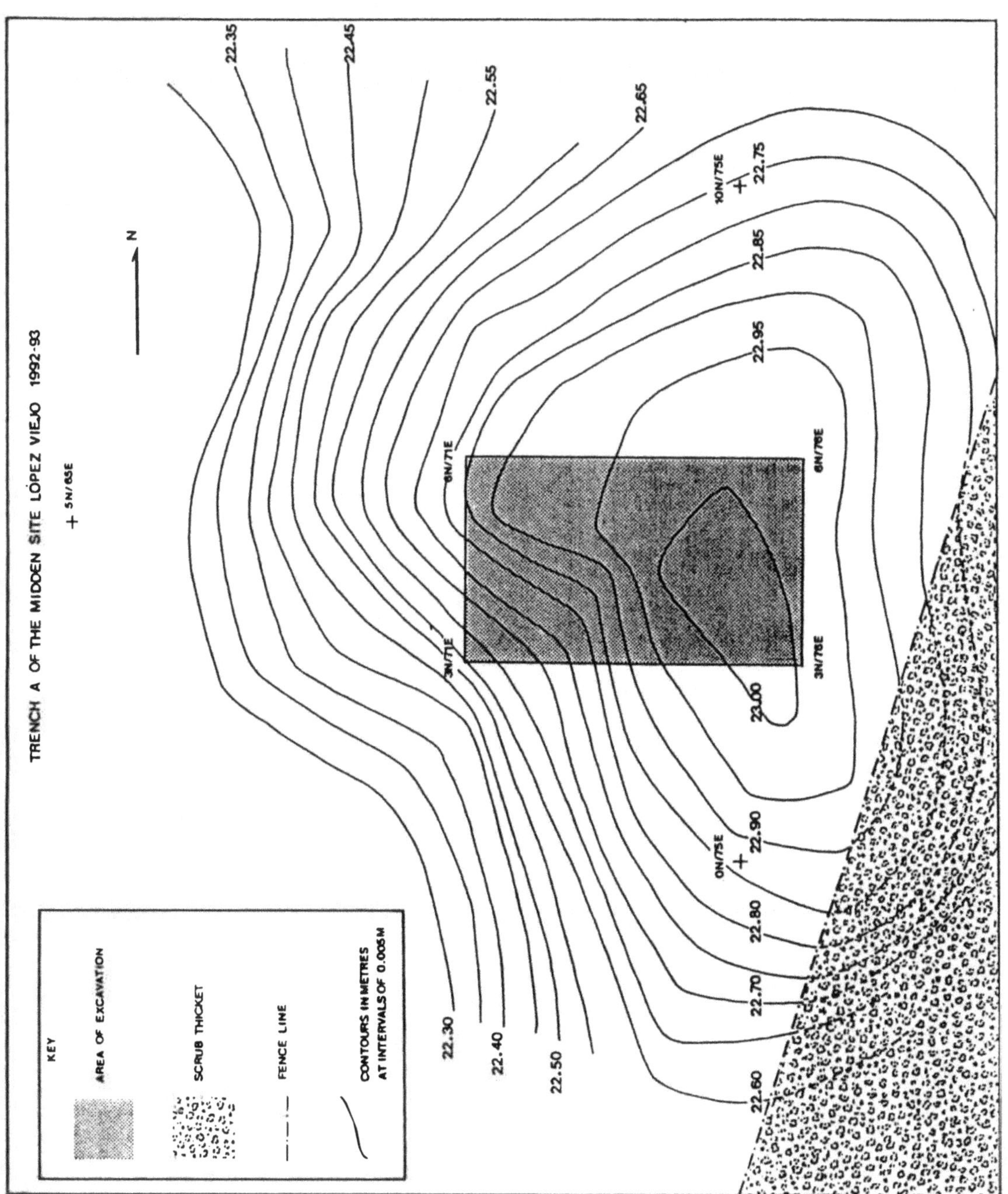

TRENCH A OF THE MIDDEN SITE LÓPEZ VIEJO 1992-93
5N/65E
N
KEY
AREA OF EXCAVATION
SCRUB THICKET
FENCE LINE
CONTOURS IN METRES AT INTERVALS OF 0.005M
22.30
22.35
22.40
22.45
22.50
22.55
22.60
22.65
22.70
22.75
22.80
22.85
22.90
22.95
23.00
3N/71E
6N/71E
3N/76E
6N/76E
0N/75E
10N/75E

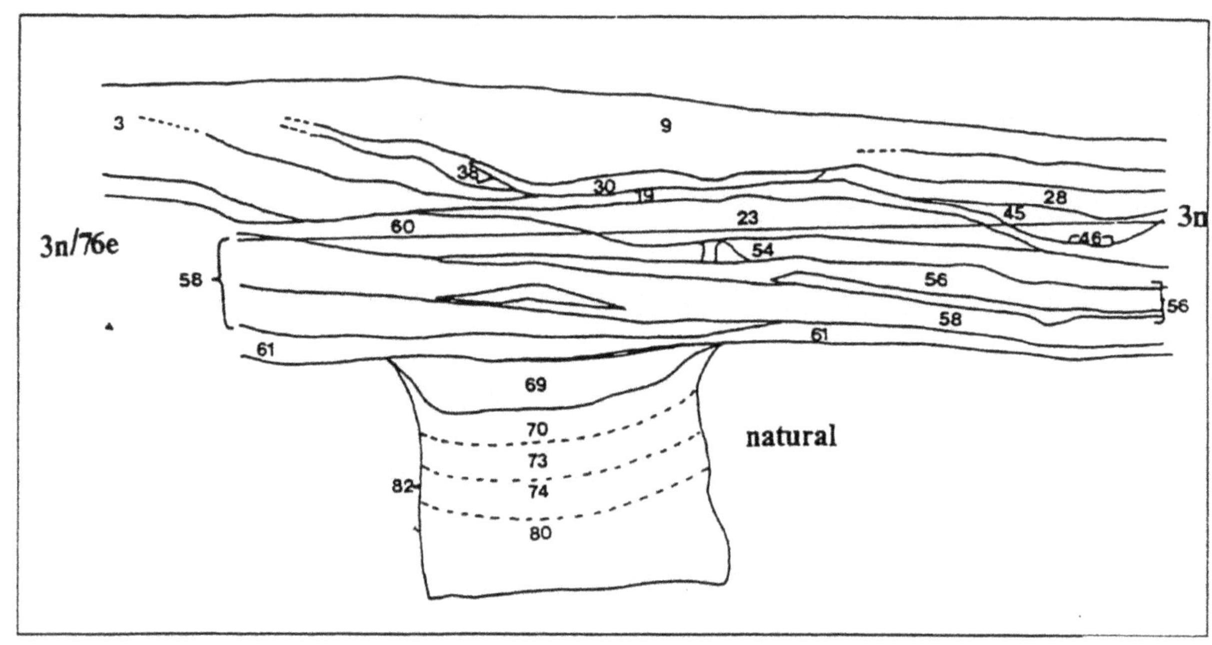

FIGURE 2 TRENCH A: 3N/71 - 76E PROFILE

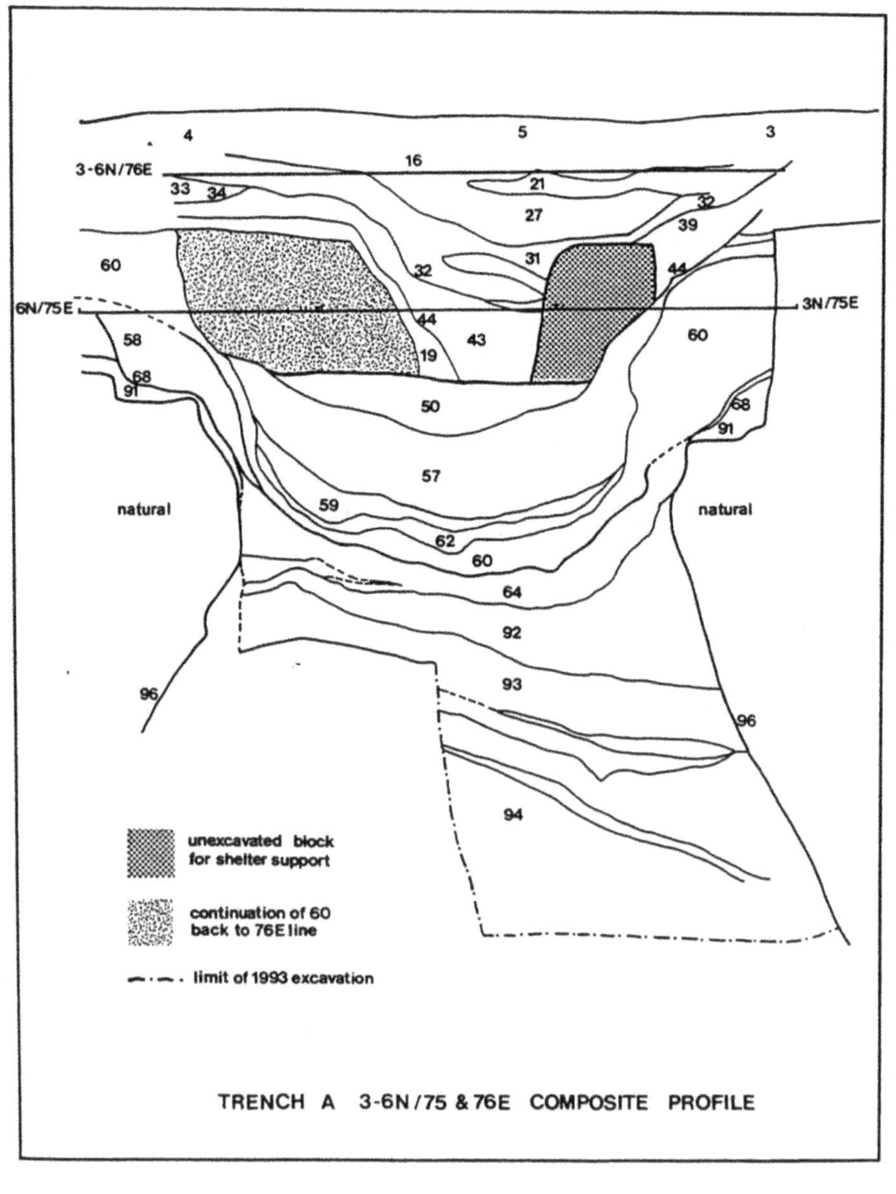

TRENCH A 3-6N/75 & 76E COMPOSITE PROFILE

FIGURE 3

The Midden Site, facing N towards Avenida Ocho

The Midden Site, facing NNW towards Avenida Ocho and Calle Ondos

Given the very dry and powdery nature of the upper midden deposits, and their lack of distinctive colour or clarity, it was decided early on to transport water to the site daily in order to keep the sediments damp during excavation. This allowed subtle colour and textual distinctions to be observed, which were completely lost if the deposits were allowed to dry out. Later contexts containing much heavy textured, crumbly, redeposited natural sediments were sometimes excavated dry.

All excavated sediment was screened through fine mesh screens (1/4 and 1/8th cm mesh). This was particularly important given the very large number of small special artifacts of shell, chert, bone and copper which constitute a major part of the finds inventory from this site. All pottery, shell, bone, chert and sandstones were kept for further study by different specialists. Sediment samples from the deposits were taken for environmental analysis and retrieval of carbonized plant remains. Carbon samples for radiocarbon dating were taken from contexts where appropriate.

Specialists in the study of marine shells (Kathleen E Clark) and archaeological bones (Patrick C Gay) worked concurrently with the excavations, advising on modifications of excavation or sampling strategies as deemed necessary, and are currently still analysing the very large quantities of faunal remains from the two sites. A lithics specialist (Gerardo Castro) has finished studying the stone artifacts and is due to present his report.

ARCHAEOLOGICAL CONTEXTS

Trench A (3–6N/71–76E) (Figure 1)

Excavation proceeded to a depth of between 0.70 and 1.20 metres throughout much of the 3 x 5 metre unit, except in the southeast end, where the presence of several recut pits of the Manteño period took excavation to a total depth of nearly 4.0 metres.

At first, little clear stratigraphy could be determined, the uppermost deposits uniformly consisting of very fine grey silty sediments containing much broken pottery, shell, chert, stone and bone. The profiles suggested a topmost humus horizon of some 5 – 10cm depth, with much root and animal disturbance (scorpions and lizards), succeeded by around 20cm of fine silty sediments, leached of mineral content into their present light greyish brown colour (Munsell 10YR 5/2). Until true stratigraphic contexts were encountered, the excavated material was therefore located within metre square sub–units, and within arbitrary contexts, measured by level. At first, occasional very patchy lenses of ashier material approximated to the only stratigraphic contexts encountered (context #s 1 – 23), but their boundary horizons were very unclear. Later, clearer textural and colour differences were encountered in the succeeding contexts, making it easier to recognise the archaeological stratigraphy. Table 1 summarises the record of archaeological contexts for Trench A. All special artifacts were recorded individually and given three–dimensional locations within the unit.

Context #s 2, 4, 6, 7, 8, 10 and 17 were all characterised by two principal qualities: when dry they were uniformly very soft, powdery and loosely compacted with a Munsell soil colour value of 10YR 6/2 light brownish grey. However, when wetted, they changed to a more moderately compacted, smooth and 'cheesy' consistency, with Munsell colours in the yellowish brown range, excepting where silvery grey patches of ashier lenses intruded. All these contexts are arbitrary, as it was impossible to recognise clear boundary horizons to distinguish them from the surrounding or underlying deposits. The best interpretation that can be given is that they all represent depositions of different 'dumps' of midden material, weathered and compacted through time. Middens of this nature are notoriously difficult to excavated for this reason.

These same contexts are apparently composed of very fine silty sediments with a high percentage of clay (clayey silt, Spence, 1990:fig 14), in proportions approximating to 50% silt, 40% clay and 10% very fine sand, with variations within these ranges. They contain varying quantities of pottery, shell, bone, and lithic material, but total archaeological finds generally account for between 10% to about 30% of the deposits. These characteristics have been excluded from Table 1 for brevity. Unless otherwise stated, archaeological material of pottery sherds, shells, bones and lithic material is found in moderate quantities throughout the deposits. Where unusually large or small quantities of any one finds group occurs, this is noted.

PRELIMINARY SUMMARY OF THE OCCUPATION AT THE MIDDEN SITE: LóPEZ VIEJO

Introduction

Analysis of the record of archaeological contexts and the inventory of special artifacts, together with preliminary observations of the pottery deriving from these contexts during the course of the excavations, gives the following sequence of events for the occupation associated with Trench A of the Midden Site, OMJPLP15, López Viejo.

Summary of the main occupation phases by context

1a) Excavation of burial cut #81 and interment of burial #79 during an unknown period, but probably late Engoroy.

1b) Construction of a small structure of unknown type within the area of later floor #72, evidenced by stake/post holes #s 84, 86, 88, 90. It is not yet possible to determine which of the burial or the stake holes are earlier. Aside from some indication of 'trample' of a few pottery sherds and shells into the natural clay surface of this area, there is no real evidence of an occupation horizon associated with the stake holes or the burial.

3) Floor #72 constructed directly over the trampled natural clay, the stake holes and the burial during the late Engoroy period, crushing the remains of the skeleton #79 *in situ*.

4) Re–occupation and floor repairs during the Guangala/Manteño period transition. During this period the floor surface was disturbed by four early Manteño period cuts (#s 68, 71, 82 and 93). The excavation of the cut for the wattle–drying oven #67 disturbed the earlier burial, truncating the legs above the knees, and the hands above the wrists. Parts of the floor surface were relaid, giving a smooth and even appearance to the surface of the later floor #61.

5) Cutting of a deep pit cut #96, probably a bell–shaped shaft tomb of the Manteño period, in the eastern end of the trench, subsequently infilled with a complex sequence of well–compacted clay and softly compacted ash fills. These contexts were not fully excavated, and any interment and associated deposits have yet to be discovered.

6) Construction of a large structure to the east of Trench A, evidenced by the deliberate laying down of a number of thick (0.50 m) layers of sterile yellow clay and gravel (redeposited natural #s 58, 56 and 60). There is evidence that this event also infilled the still partially open pit cut #96, with its sequence of fills #s 64, 93, 92, 91 and 64.

7) The mound of yellow redeposited natural was augmented by another thick layer of yellow clay #54. These layers of yellow clay have been reported as favoured by the Manteño people in the construction of artificial house mounds (R. Lunnis, personal communication).

8) An apparently long phase of occupation then took place, probably associated with the structure to the east of Trench A, on a prominent mound in this area. Context #23 consists of many narrow, ill–defined occupation and dumping layers, consistent with an interpretation of refuse dumping down the outer edge of the occupation mound.

9) Accumulated refuse of #23 was cut out on the east side of the trench by the cut #63 step to a pit or well still existing in the eastern end of the trench.

10) A complex sequence of pit recuts and successive fills is then observed in the contextual record, and it seems likely that there was a long history of use of a storage or refuse pit here. For example, a clay pit lining #41 may well indicate that the pit was used for water storage at one time.

11) Dumping of an extensive layer of burned material #19 partially infilling the latest pit.

12) A final sequence of occupation and dumping layers context #s 1 – 18.

The latest phases of site usage will not be documented owing to the considerable erosional effects of successive Niño rains through time, which have swept much of the latest phases of the prehistoric occupation of this hillside down into the erosion gullies below. It is not known at what point the site was abandoned, but it seems likely that occupation at López Viejo continued more or less unbroken up to modern times, whilst the main locus of settlement for any one period moved around the overall site. The present modern occupation of the hilltop here in the Barrio Míramar is apparently a fairly recent extension eastward from the modern town, yet earlier surveys show that a settlement of considerable size with many structures existed here, possibly until the Conquest. Further survey and excavation in the area may well clarify this question.

Conclusion

The sequence of occupation of the Trench A site outlined above is based principally upon the analysis of the contextual record. Reference to archaeological cultures such as Engoroy, Guangala and Manteño are provisional, and it would be expected that this summary will be modified and developed following a detailed analysis of the ceramic record in the second stage of post– excavation analysis planned to take place in 1994.

TABLE 1

Context Number	Grid	Brief Description of Context	Interpretation	Method
1	3-5N/73-75E	Well-compacted deposit: Munsell 10YR3/3 Dark Brown	Last midden dump	Trowel
2*	5-6N/71-74E	Soft, loosely compacted deposit: 10YR 3/4-5/6, dark yellowish brown - yellowish brown silty clay, with ashy grey lenses and charcoal; dense concentrations of pottery and shell (>25% of deposit)	One of final weathered & compacted deposits	Trowel
3*	3-5N/73-76E	Moderate - softly compacted deposit: 10YR3/4 dark yellowish brown, clayey silt with fine sand and occasional charcoal	Dumped midden deposit	Trowel
4*	5-6N/74-76E	Soft, loosely compacted deposit, cohesive when wet: 10YR3/4 dark yellowish brown, with lenses of ashy material, 4/2 dark greyish brown, fine silty sediment with clay and frequent charcoal inclusions	Dumped midden deposit	Trowel
5*	4-5N/75-76E	Soft, loosely compacted deposit: 10YR3/4-4/4 dark yellowish brown, fine silty sediment with clay and frequent charcoal inclusions	Dumped midden deposit	Trowel
6*	3-5N/71-73E	Ranges from hard-loosely compacted deposit: 10YR4/4 dark yellowish brown, clayey silt	Dumped midden deposit	Trowel
7*	5-6N/71-74E	Softly compacted deposit: 10YR5/3 brown - 3/3 dark brown clayey silt, patchy lenses & pockets of ashy sediment, similar to context 2 above, but with fewer finds	Dumped midden deposit	Trowel
8*	5-6N/74-75E	Soft, loosely compacted deposit: 10YR 4/4 greyish brown, clayey silt	Dumped midden deposit	Trowel
9	3-4N/71-76E	Soft, loosely compacted deposit: 10YR 3/3 dark brown, clayey silt with some fine sand and dense ashy lenses. Many small bones, large land snails and large concentrations of urchin spines	Dumped midden deposit	Trowel
10*	5-6N/71-73E	Varies from lightly to very loosely compacted deposit: 10YR 7/4-6/2 in patches, clayey silt with ashier silvery grey lenses, frequent inclusions of reddish brown burned clay and charcoal fragments. Many valves of *P.sterna*	Dumped midden deposit	Trowel
11*	3-5N/71-75E	Varies from well-moderately compacted and 'cheesy'deposit: 10YR 3/4 - 4/4 dark yellowish brown - 5/3 brown, silty clay with very fine sand, frequent inclusions of charcoal & burned clay fragments	Dumped midden deposit	TrowelPla st. leaf
12*	4-6N/74-76E	Varies from soft, loosely compacted to moderately compacted 'cheesy' deposit: 10YR5/2 greyish brown - 6/2 light brownish grey and yellow where burned clay occurs, clayey silt with ashy lenses, frequent inclusions of charcoal and burned clay	Earlier midden deposit	Trowel Plast. leaf
13	4-5N/74-75E	Varies from soft and loose to moderately compacted deposit: 10YR 3/2 very dark greyish brown, and yellow, fine soft sediment with much charcoal and ash, and patches of fine sand	Equivalent to #19, intruding through from beneath	Trowel and leaf
14	4-5N/73-74E	Very soft & loosely compacted deposit: 10YR 3/2 very dark greyish brown & 7.5YR 6/8 reddish yellow, very fine clayey silt with ash and fine yellow sand, frequent charcoal inclusions, small bones and chert flakes	Equivalent to #19 intruding through from beneath	Trowel and leaf
15	3-5N/74-76E	Very compacted deposit: 10YR 5/4 - 4/4 yellowish brown - dark yellowish brown silty clay with some fine sand, patches of grey ashy material	Recut pit fill or clay pit lining	Trowel and leaf
16	3-5N/72-76E	Moderately compacted deposit: 10YR 5/4 yellowish brown - 4/4 dark yellowish brown, clay and fine sand with powdery ash lenses, frequent inclusions of charcoal and burned clay, also many chert flakes	Possible dumped deposit	Trowel and leaf
17	5-6N/73-76E	Moderately compacted deposit: 10YR 6/6 brownish yellow where baked clay occurs, 7/2 & 3/2 very dark greyish brown where ash and charcoal lenses occur, sandy clay & silt with frequent charcoal & burned clay	Possible surface where organic material was burned, or dumped after burning	Trowel and leaf
18	3-4N/72-76E	Moderately compacted deposit: 10YR yellowish brown silty clay with fine sand, small ashy patches and charcoal flecks. Finds infrequent, but many urchin spines in ashy lenses	Possible dumped deposit	Trowel and leaf
19	3-6N/71-76E	Loose to moderately compacted deposit: 10YR 3/2 very dark greyish brown with occasional lenses of 8/1 white & 7/8 yellow, mixed sediment of clayey silt with much charcoal and occasional very fine sand, much pottery and urchin spines	Pit and cut fill, partially removed by later pit recuts (eg #s44 & 46)	Trowel and leaf
20	3-5N/75-76E	Very loose deposit: 10YR5/3 brown composed of </60% chert flakes, cores & debitage in a 40% silty clay with fine sand matrix with few other finds	Chert working area and dump	Trowel and leaf
21	3-5N/74-76E	Initially hard compacted, breaks to loose deposit: 10YR 7/1 - 7/2 light grey to 3/2 very dark greyish brown ashy sediment with some fine sand, occasional charcoal, burned clay and many urchin spines	Ash dump	Trowel
22	4-6N/74-76E	Loosely compacted deposit: 10YR 5/3 - 5/4 brown to yellowish brown silty clay with fine sand, one small light grey ashy lens, frequent small bones & shells	Dumped deposit	Trowel
23	3-6N/71-75E	Moderately compacted, 'cheesy' deposit: varies from 10YR 5/4 yellowish brown - 7/2 light grey - 6/6 brownish yellow, silty clay with </20% fine sand & </20% ash, frequent inclusions of charcoal & many shells of sp *Olivella*, many chert flakes & debitage, many small bones and a lens of urchin bodies & spines, large concentrations of pottery, shell and 'specials' eg grooved tubular beads	>/0.50 m compacted midden dump containing poorly defined horizons of possible floor trample areas	Trowel and leaf

Context Number	Grid	Brief Description of Context	Interpretation	Method
24	4-6N/74-76E	Moderately compacted deposit: 10YR 3/3 dark brown, clayey silt with >/20% fine sand containing much pottery, oyster shells, urchin spines, but little chert. Special finds of worked oyster	Dumped or accumulated deposit	Trowel and leaf
25	4-6N/73-76E	Moderately compacted deposit: 10YR 5/3 brown - 5/4 yellowish brown silty clay with </10% fine sand, poorly defined boundaries, many small fish bones and small gastropod shells	Composite of dumped lenses of refuse	Trowel
26	4-6N/73-75E	Loosely compacted deposit: 10YR 5/3 brown, with occasional 5/1 grey & 7/1 light grey ash lenses, slightly sandy silt with frequent small round stones, occasional large pot sherds, many small bones, moderate shell & urchin spines	Dumped midden deposit	Trowel
27	3-6N/72-76E	Moderately compacted cohesive deposit: 2.5YR 4/2 greyish brown with 2.5 6/2 light brownish grey, silty clay with </20% fine sand, occasional sand & ash lenses, frequent charcoal flecks, flattened pot sherds, shell & burned clay, many urchin spines & body parts associated with ashy patches, occasional large rounded cobbles	Dumped midden deposit with evidence of floor trample in some areas; partial fill to #32	Trowel
28	3-4N/73-74E	Loosely compacted deposit: 10YR 5/3 brown - 5/4 yellowish brown, clayey silt with </10% fine sand, many small angular stones, occasional large rounded stones, little pot, shell, bone	Recut fill or partial lining to large pit #44	Trowel
29	3-6N/74-76E	Loosely compacted deposit: 10YR 5/2 greyish brown with patches of 7/2 & 6/2 light grey & greyish brown, mixed silty clay with </10% fine sand, frequent charcoal & shells	One of 3 fills to cut #32	Trowel
30	3-4N/72-75E	Moderately compacted deposit: 10YR 2/2 - 2/1 very dark brown to black, very fine silty sediment with much carbon, little archaeological material, except urchin spines with an associated ashy lens	Fill to shallow cut feature #38	Trowel
31	3-6N/74-76E	Moderately compacted cohesive deposit: 10YR 5/3 brown, 5/1 grey with charcoal, 7/1 grey without charcoal, occasional 8/6 yellow, heterogeneous deposit of silty clay with </10% fine sand, frequent charcoal, shells, bones, chert flakes & cores, burned clay and whole pearl oyster shells	One of 3 fills to pit, cut #32	Trowel
32	3-6N/74-76E	Irregular sub-circular cut, 2.30 x 1.60 m, 64cm deep, with approximately rounded corners and sharp slope break, stepped - steep gradient sides, sharp slope break at base, with gently sloping floor	Pit, probably for refuse, poss. re-used water-storage?	
33	5-6N/74-76E	Loose deposit under well-compacted surface: 10YR 5/3 brown with occasional 5/2 greyish brown, 5/8 yellowish brown & 8/3 very pale brown, slightly clayey silt with >/10% fine sand, many small bones, shell & potsherds, frequent small rounded stones and chert flakes	Fill of shallow cut feature #34	Trowel
34	5-6N/74-76E	Irregular sub-circular cut, 1.15 x 0.60 m, 4-15cm deep, with rounded corner, sharp slope break at top, gently sloping sides and sides at base to flat bottom. Truncated by other feature: little survives	Shallow cut ? refuse pit	
35	3-5N/74-76E	Irregular, extensively truncated, sub-rectangular cut, 1.90 x 1.60 m, 63cm deep, with one surviving rounded corner, sharp slope-break at top, slopes with some stepping directly into base, sharp to bottom	Truncated/recut pit (by #32)	
36	3-5N/73-76E	Loosely compacted deposit: 10YR 5/3 brown with constant flecks of 6/6 brownish yellow & black carbon flecks, one ash patch of 5/1 grey, clayey silt with </10% fine sand, frequent charcoal and coral fragments, occasional potsherd, shell & bone	Fill of shallow cut feature #37	Trowel
37	3-5N/73-75E	Approximately linear cut, 2.60 x 1 m, 12-21cm deep, with truncated edges, no corners, gradual slope break at top with gently sloping sides, sharp slope-break at base with flat - gently sloping bottom	Shallow cut, possibly a gulley into pit cut #35	
38	3-4N/72-75E	Sub-rectangular cut, 1.80 x 0.20 m, 5-10cm deep, with one long edge & two rounded corners, gradual slope-break top, smoothly sloping sides to no recognisable base	Shallow filled cut	
39	3-5N/74-76E	Loosely compacted heterogeneous deposit, 10yr 7/2 light grey, 5/1 grey amidst 5/3 & 5/4 brown and yellowish brown matrix, slightly clayey silt with </10% fine sand, much pottery and small bones	Recut fill to cut feature, probably pit	Trowel
40	3-5N/74-76E	Loosely compacted heterogeneous deposit: 10YR 5/3 brown, with 7/1 & 5/1 light grey & grey at base, slightly sandy silt, fine sand </10%, many potsherds, frequent small bones and many urchin spines, little oyster shell	One of 4 fills to pit cut #44	Trowel
41	4-6N/74-76E	Well-compacted cohesive deposit: 10YR 7/4 very pale brown, with occasional 8/6 yellow, silty clay with </5% fine sand, with occasional finds	Clay lining to pit cut #44	Trowel and pick
42	3-5N/74-76E	Loosely compacted heterogeneous deposit: 10YR 5/1 grey, with 6/6 brownish yellow & 6/4 light yellowish brown sandy silt with frequent small bones & occasional other finds	Small remnant fill to pit cut #44	Trowel
43	4-6N/74-76E	Moderately compacted deposit: 10YR 5/3 brown - 6/3 pale brown, occasional 3/1 very dark grey, silty clay with fine sand, frequent inclusions of charcoal and lime, many potsherds, bones, urchin parts, occasional other finds	One of 4 fills to pit cut #44	Trowel
44	3-6N/74-76E	Irregular sub-circular shaped cut, 2.40 x 1.80 m, 95cm deep, with sharp slope-break at top, irregular sides sloping directly or stepped to a partially overhung flat base	Pit cut	
45	3-4N/71-73E	Loosely compacted deposit: 10YR 6/2 greyish brown dry powdery sediment of slightly sandy clay & silt, very frequent chert cores, flakes & debitage, infrequent pottery, shells & bones	Fill to pit cut #46	Trowel
46	3-4N/71-73E	Irregular truncated cut, 1.30 x 0.50 m, 27cm deep, with sharp slope break at top, concave sides, sloping gently into concave base & no discernable bottom	Pit cut	

Context Number	Grid	Brief Description of Context	Interpretation	Method
47	3-4N/71-76E	Loosely compacted deposit but cohesive when wet: 10YR 7/2 light grey with patches of 5/3 brown, clayey silt with fine sand </10%, frequent small pebbles, occasional other finds	Long linear deposit of dumped midden material	Trowel
48	3-4N/75-76E	Moderately compacted, cohesive deposit: 10YR brown, silty clay with </10% coarse sand, occasional pot, chert cores & small bones, frequent urchin spines	Fill to cut feature #49, possibly refuse pit	Trowel
49	3-4N/75-76E	Irregular sub-rectangular cut, 0.90 x 0.60 m, 39cm deep, no surviving corners, sharp slope break at top, smooth - stepped sides, sharp slope break into remains of flat base	Shallow cut ?refuse pit	
50	3-6N/73-76E	Loosely compacted deposit: 10YR 5/3 brown with 5/4 yellowish brown, 6/2 brownish grey & 7/1 light grey clayey silt with </20% fine sand, frequent shell, small bones, chert flakes & urchin spines	Second fill of long shallow cut #63 into natural clay	Trowel
51	3-4N/71-72E	Loosely compacted deposit: 10YR 5/3 brown clayey silt with </10% fine sand, occasional finds	One of two fills to small cut feature #55	Trowel
52	3-4N/71-72E	Loosely compacted deposit: 10YR 5/2 greyish brown and yellow (no Munsell value) powdery sediment of slightly clayey silt with </5% sand, very few finds of all kinds, but frequent angular stones	Redeposited natural	Trowel
53	3-4N/71-72E	Loose and crumbly, very dry deposit: 10YR 6/2 light brownish grey with 2.5 Y 7/6 & 6/6 yellow & olive yellow clayey silt with </10% sand mixed with natural sediment ratio 60:40, few finds	Fill to pit cut #55 containing a proportion of redeposited natural	Trowel
54	3-6N/71-75E	Loosely compacted deposit, cohesive when wet: 10YR 5/3 brown gravely sediment of clayey silt with </10% fine sand, very frequent small stones and frequent urchin spines and bleached out shells	Dumped or accumulated deposit, open to air over time	Trowel & pick
55	3-4N/71-72E	Sub-circular cut, 0.60 x 0.55 m, 65cm deep, sharp slope break at top, some edges near vertical to sharp break into flat bottom	Small cut pit	
56	3-6N/71-75E	Loosely compacted crumbly deposit, cohesive wet: 10YR 5/3 brown, clayey silt with very little fine sand, few finds of pot, bone & lithics	Dumped deposit	Pick
57	3-6N/74-76E	Well-compacted clay & lightly compacted ash deposit: 10yr 5/6 yellowish brown - 2.5 6/2 light brownish grey composite fills, consisting of clay with lime (80:20%) and ash, frequent small pieces compacted clay, many urchin parts associated with ash, many bones & potsherds	Combination of </two pit fills to pit cut #68	Trowel and pick
58	3-6N/71-73E	Moderately compacted deposit: 2.5YR 5/4 light olive brown - 6/8 olive yellow clay with small angular stones (gravel?) & some silt (60:20:20), very few finds, some bleached shells	Thick, deliberately laid dump of redeposited natural sediment	Pick and trowel
59	3-6N/74-76E	Composite of four fills: a) 10YR 3/6 dark yellowish brown well-compacted clay with 10% lime; b) 10YR 5/4 yellowish brown semi-compacted clay with much ash & organic material; 5Y 7/2 light grey ash with very fine water-laid sedimentary horizons; d) 10YR 3/1 dark yellowish brown lime & clay with particles of white ash & small stones. Overall many urchin parts, bones & lithics, less potsherd	Complex of four different fills to pit cut #68	Pick and trowel
60	3-6N/73-76E	Loosely compacted deposit, crumbly when dry: 2.5Y 7/4 pale yellow - 5/4 light olive brown gravel within a clayey silt matrix, very occasional finds of shell & potsherd	Redeposited natural sediment from excavation of a large pit, or continuous lining	Pick and trowel
61	3-6N/71-72E	Very hard compacted deposit surface over loose and crumbly under matrix: 10YR 5/3 brown, sandy silt with clay & some ash, frequent potsherd & shell, occasional urchin parts & bone; ashy lens contained much polished blackware pottery	Fill or repair to a shallow cut in secure floor deposit #72	Pick and trowel
62	3-6N/74-76E	Well-compacted deposit: 10YR 5/3 yellowish brown, </90% fine clay with lenses of lime and ash	Intentional waterproof lining of pit bottom	Trowel
63	3-6N/74-75E	Long shallow sub-circular cut, 2.60 x 0.20 m, 30cm deep, with steep edges, base removed by later pit recuts	? 'Step' down into storage pit or well	
64	3-6N/74-76E	Softly compacted composite deposit: a) 5Y 5/1 grey b) 10YR 8/1 white & 10YR 5/4 yellowish brown & 3/6 dark yellowish brown, ash layers & clay with gravel (60:40%), with frequent carbon	Fills to large deep pit cut #96	Trowel
65	5-6N/71-72E	Very softly compacted: 10YR 6/2 light brownish grey ash with lime powder & clay (40:60%)	Fill to oven #67	Spoon and trowel
66	4-6N/71-74E	Loosely compacted deposit: 10yr 5/3 brown clayey silt with </5% coarse sand and few finds	Repairs to floor #61	Trowel
67	5-6N#71-72E	Hard baked deposit: 5YR 6/8 reddish yellow & 2.5YR 6/8 light red - 5/8 . red of fine burned clay	Wattle drying oven	Trowel
68	3-6N/74-76E	Large, sub-circular shallow cut, 2.80 x 0.50 m with steep slope break into nearly vertical sides and sharp slop break into flat base, one 'correction' to angle of cut visible	Possibly cut to widen the aperture/access of the pit #96	
69	3-4N/73-75E	Well-compacted deposit: 10YR 7/3 very pale brown (dry) silty clay with 5-10% sand, occasional charcoal flecks and few finds	Shallow fill to pit cut #82	Trowel
70	3-4N/73-75E	Loosely compacted lumpy deposit: 2.5Y 5/4 light olive brown silty clay with </10% fine sand, few finds	Fill to pit cut #82	Trowel and dry
71	5-6N/71-72E	Sub-circular, double chamber 'hourglass' cut, 0.55 m, 56 cm deep, with steep & concave sides in upper & lower sections & with concave shallow 'dish' shaped base	Cut for double wattle-drying oven #67	

Context Number	Grid	Brief Description of Context	Interpretation	Method
72	4-6N/71-75	Moderately to well compacted on surface, crumbly deposit, 10-20cm deep: 10YR 5/3 brown - 5/2 greyish brown (dry), clayey silt with </10% charcoal & </10% fine sand, abundant pottery fragments, but few shells, bones or lithics	Well prepared level surface, ?Engoroy floor	Trowel and pick, dry
73	3-4N/73-75E	Softly compacted, powdery deposit: 7.5YR 6/2 pinkish grey (dry) clayey silt with </15% fine sand, frequent inclusions of charcoal & lumps of yellow redeposited natural sediment, abundant finds, including much burned shell	Third fill to pit cut #82	Trowel dry
74	3-4N/73-75E	Loosely compacted, crumbly deposit: 10YR 7/2 light grey (dry) clayey silt with </10% sand & </10% ash, frequent chunks of redeposited yellow natural sediment & charcoal flecks, occasional patches of charcoal and powdery ash	Fourth fill to pit cut #82	Pick, dry
75	4-6N/71-72E	Loose unconsolidated, rubbly: 10YR 5/3 brown clayey silt with </ 15% sand, some burned clay, few finds	Fill to burial #79	Trowel spoon
76	3-4N/73-75	No information: redundant context?		
77	5-6N/72-73E	Very loose & unconsolidated powdery deposit: 10YR 5/2 greyish brown (dry), clayey silt with <20% fine sand	Fill to stake hole #78	Hand and spoon
78	5-6N/72-73E	Oval shaped, 0.15 x 0.08 m, </25cm deep cut with smooth vertical sides, orientated N-S	Stake hole	
79	4-6N/71-72E	Human skeleton deposit: orientated head SW - legs NE, truncated below upper femurs & below lower ulna/radius, through cut for oven #71. Poor condition, crushed & flattened skull, probably through pressure from floor #72 above. ?Young adult female, with one stone bead	Burial	Fine instruments of excavation
80	3-4N/73-75E	Very hard compacted deposit: 10YR 6/3 pale brown - 7.5YR 7/2 pinkish grey (dry), silty clay with </5% sand, occasional charcoal flecking, few finds	Fifth fill to pit cut #82	Trowel and pick
81	4-6N/71-72E	Sub-rectangular shallow cut, 1.35 x 0.50 m, 25cm deep for #79 (burial), with vertical sides into an irregular flat base	Burial cut for skeleton #79	Trowel
82	3-4N/73-74	Semi-circular pit cut, 1.60 x 0.80 m, 1.20 m deep, sharp slope break with top all round, stepped sides with some overhang into sharp slope break at base to flat bottom	Pit cut for ?refuse	
83	4-5N/72-73E	Moderately compacted, friable deposit: 10YR 5/3 - 5/2 brown - greyish brown (dry), clayey silt with </10% fine sand	Fill to post hole #84	Spoon and trowel
84	4-5N/72-73E	Circular cut, 10cm diameter, 13cm deep	Post hole	
85	4-5N/72-73E	Moderately compacted, friable deposit: 10YR 5/3 - 5/2 brown - greyish brown (dry), clayey silt with </10% fine sand	Fill to post hole #86	Spoon and trowel
86	4-5N/72-73E	Oval cut, 15 x 20 cm, 12cm deep	Post hole	
87	5-6N/73-74E	Moderately compacted, friable deposit: 10YR 5/3 - 5/2 brown - greyish brown (dry), clayey silt with </10% fine sand	Fill to post hole #88	Spoon and trowel
88	5-6N/73-74E	Circular cut 15cm diameter, 8cm deep	Post hole	
89	5-6N/74-75E	Moderately compacted, friable deposit: 10YR 5/3 brown - 5/2 greyish brown (dry), clayey silt with </10% fine sand	Fill to post hole #90	Spoon and trowel
90	5-6N/74-75E	Circular cut, 20cm diameter, 16cm deep	Post hole	
91	3-6N/74-76	Moderately compacted deposit: 10YR 3/4 dark yellowish brown (dry), clay with </10% lime, charcoal inclusions	Fill to deep pit #96, possibly mixed with detached pit wall (natural sediment)	Trowel
92	3-6N/74-76E	Well-compacted deposit: 10YR 5/6 yellowish brown, clay with </10% lime, well-preserved plant fibre impressions, few finds	Fill to deep pit #96	Trowel
93	3-6N/74-76E	Soft, loosely compacted deposit of two types of fill: varies in colour with fill: white & grey ash with black charcoal, contains carbonized plant and fibre remains	Composite of two ash/carbon fills to deep pit #96	Trowel
94	3-6N/74-76E	Composite context of hard compacted dark yellowish brown clay interspersed with layers of soft, very loosely compacted white and black ash	Composite of fills to deep pit #96	Trowel
95	4-6N/71-74E	Irregular, shallow cut, 20cm deep, with sloping edges and flat base	Cut/repair of floor #72	Trowel and pick
96	3-6N/74-76E	Deep sub-circular pit c 2.25 m diameter at top, with steep sides, undercutting sharply into a bell-shaped profile, contains many complex fills of ash and clay, but not 'bottomed' through reason of its great depth (</4 m from ground level at end of excavation) and shortage of time	Manteño bell-shaped shaft tomb	

* Arbitrary context

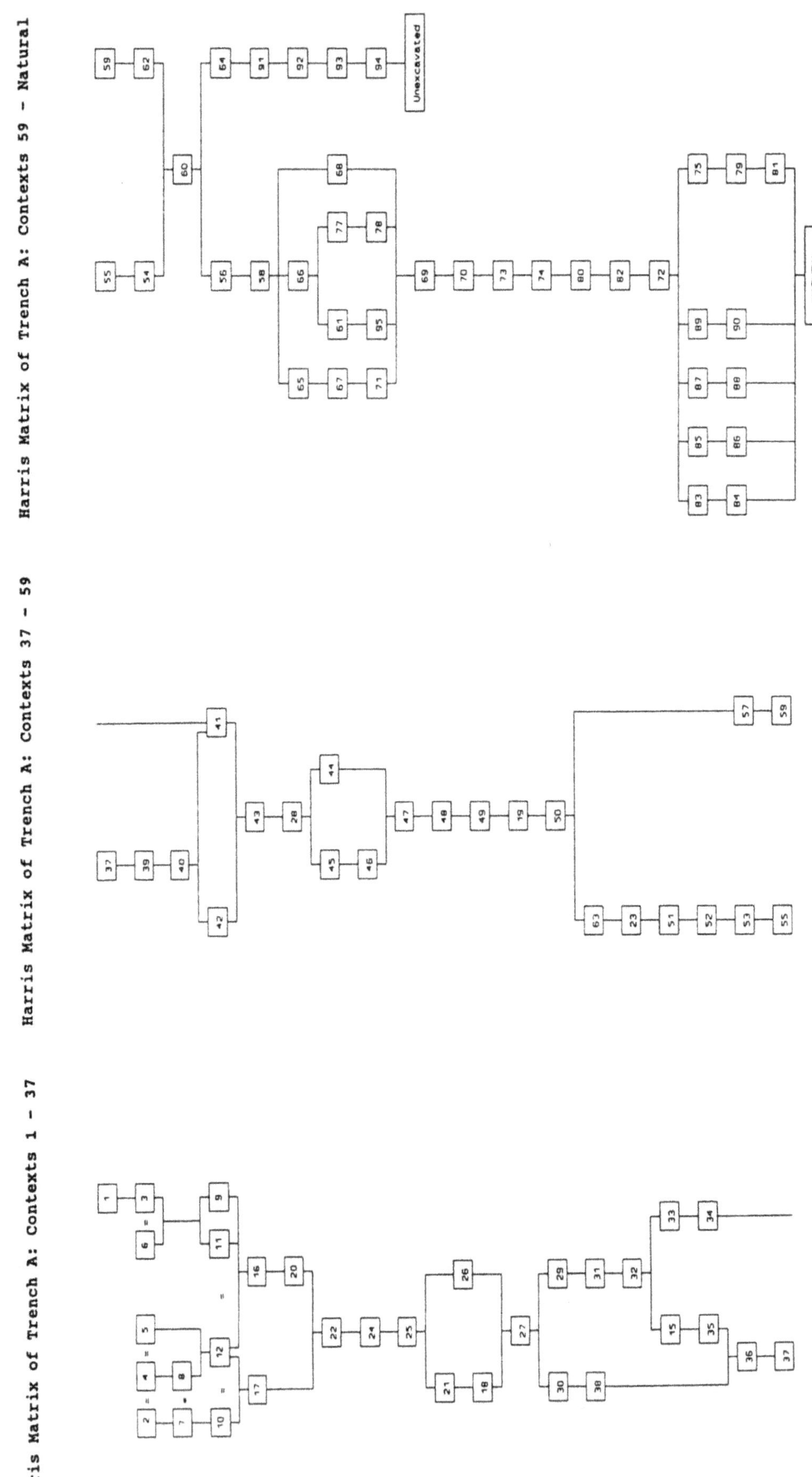
Harris Matrix of Trench A: Contexts 1 - 37
Harris Matrix of Trench A: Contexts 37 - 59
Harris Matrix of Trench A: Contexts 59 - Natural
Unexcavated
NATURAL

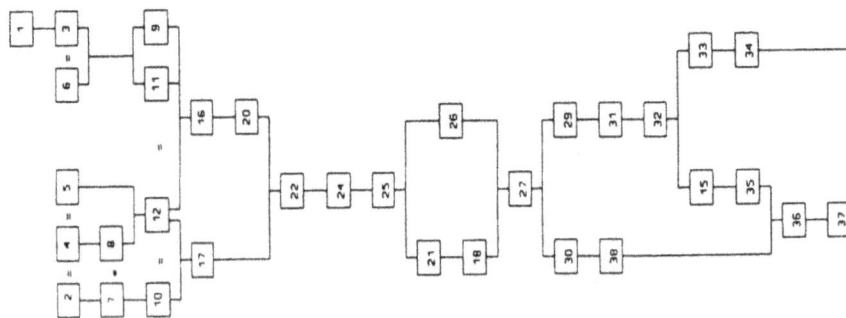

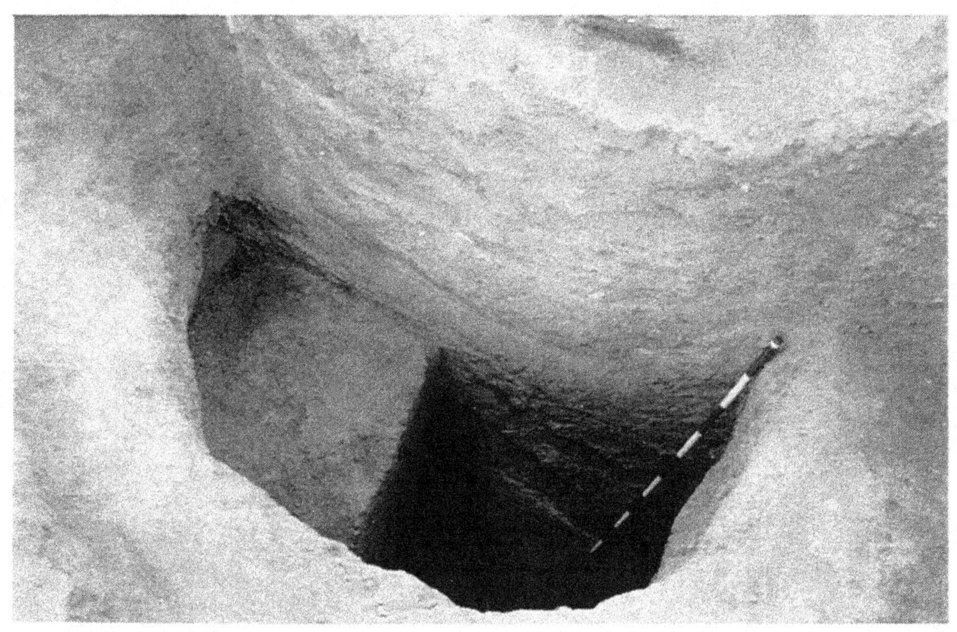

N–S Profile (W facing) of shaft grave

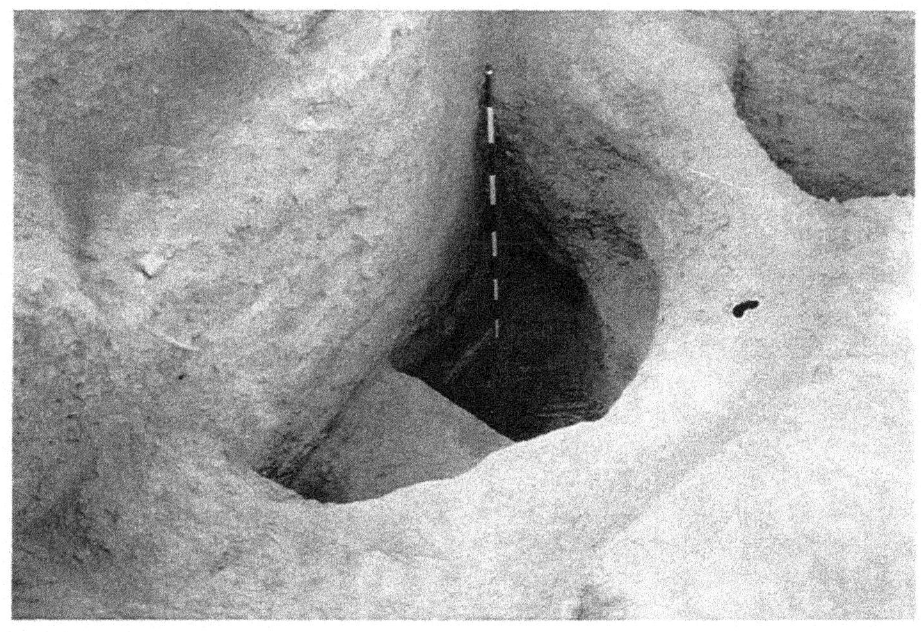

CHAPTER 3

THE FINDS

Introduction

The first stage of analysis of artifacts from López Viejo has been completed, concentrating upon the more than 2000 special artifacts excavated from Trench A (3–6N/71–76E). The proportion of special finds to "ordinary" is very high. These special artifacts may be classified within five broad categories of material: shell artifacts, particularly those fashioned from mother–of–pearl (*Pinctada mazatlanica* and *Pteria sterna*), ceramic artifacts, such as figurines and spindle whorls, copper artifacts, such as pins and awls, lithic artifacts, such as chert drills and stone net weights and finally bone artifacts, such as cut and polished segments (possibly necklace components). It will be noticed from the distribution data presented in tables 2 – 9 that many of the different categories of special artifacts, such as the chert drills, bone segments, discs and figurines tend to cluster in groups in certain of the later contexts, associated with the midden dump deposits (e.g., context #s 2, 3, 6, 7, 10, 11, 12 and 23). It is planned to carry out a statistical testing of artifact–context relationships to be presented in the next report.

Given the very large quantity of pottery found at the Midden Site, López Viejo, together with the unusually high number of special artifacts, it has been necessary to defer ceramic analysis to a second phase of post–excavation analysis in 1994, although a preliminary statement on the pottery, based upon initial observations of the pottery coming from the different units and contexts during the course of the excavations, will be dealt with under the appropriate section below.

The following section describes each category of special artifact. It should be noted, however, that given the very large number of special artifacts found, and the great variation of information to be analyzed within each sub–group, it has not been possible to carry out a very detailed level of analysis at this stage. It is planned to carry out a 'second level' analysis later, which will then facilitate statistical testing of variations of types within these groups.

It should be noted that not all special artifacts have been included in the descriptive sections which follow. Although the majority fall into one of several clearly defined groups, there are a number of 'miscellaneous' special artifacts, for example unidentifiable items of corroded copper, modified whole shells or crudely worked lithic items which, given the very large number of artifacts, have been excluded from this First Report. Similarly, there are groups described below, for example cut shell and shell drills which, owing to limitations of time, have been omitted from the tabular sections.

SHELL ARTIFACTS

There are seven main groups of artifacts within this overall heading: discs, crescents, ornaments, figures, cut shell, beads and tools. The great majority of shell special artifacts are fashioned from the pearl oyster, *P. mazatlanica*, with a very few others manufactured from *Pteria Sterna* and *Spondylus* spp. Then there are occasional modified whole shells of other species, which are not discussed here, but which will be included with a more detailed analysis of the special shell artifacts and related shell–working technology in a subsequent report.

Shell Discs (Table 2)

Shell discs form one of the most common groups of shell special artifacts from the site. These, in turn, may be sub–divided into 7 different groups:

1) whole plain discs, with no evidence of any further working;
2) whole discs marked in the centre of either one or other side (rarely both) with small 'peck' marks presumably in preparation for boring;
3) semi–bored discs, with central perforations incomplete;
4) whole discs with completed central perforations, usually made from the inner side of the valve;
5) plain half discs, deliberately sliced in two;
6) half discs with semi–circular marks upon one side (usually the inside) of the valve, or with a semi–circular portion cut out of the centre;
7) Fine discs: wafer–thin smoothly rounded discs, well– finished on both sides, either bored with one perforation through the centre, or with one perforation through the 'top', possibly for use as a pendant ornament;
8) disc fragments of any of the above groups, probably accidental fractures.

P. mazatlanica. Centre–marked Disc (2/3 size)

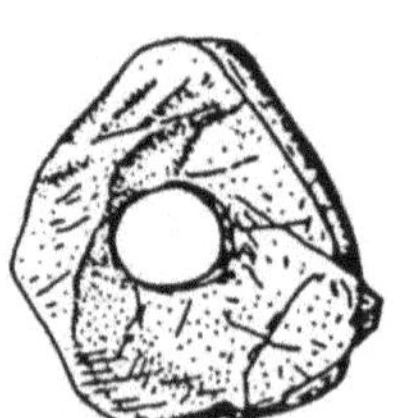

P. mazatlanica. Centre–bored Disc (2/3 size)

TABLE 2: SHELL DISCS											
CONTEXT	COMPLETE			HALF			FRAGMENTS			FINE DISCS	
	pla	bor	ma	pla	bor	cut	pla	cut	ma	cen bor	top bor
None	1	0	0	1	0	0	0	0	0	0	0
2	5	0	0	0	0	0	0	0	1	0	0
3	5	1	2	0	0	2	1	0	0	0	1
4	1	0	0	1	0	0	0	0	0	0	0
5	0	0	0	0	0	0	0	0	0	1	0
6	2	0	3	1	1	0	1	0	0	0	1
7	2	1	0	0	0	1	0	2	0	1	0
8	1	0	0	0	0	0	0	0	0	0	0
9	1	0	0	1	0	0	1	0	0	0	0
10	0	0	0	0	0	0	0	0	0	1	0
11	3	1	1	0	0	0	0	1	0	0	0
12	2	0	0	2	0	0	0	0	0	1	0
16	0	0	0	1	0	0	1	1	0	0	0
17	0	1	0	0	0	0	0	0	0	0	0
18	1	0	0	0	0	1	0	1	0	0	0
19	3	1	0	0	1	0	0	0	0	0	1
21	0	0	0	0	0	0	0	0	0	1	0
22	1	0	0	0	0	0	0	0	0	0	0
23	6	1	3	2	0	3	1	2	0	0	1
25	1	1	1	0	0	1	0	0	0	0	0
27	0	1	0	0	0	1	0	0	0	0	0
29	1	0	0	0	0	1	0	1	0	0	0
31	0	0	2	0	0	0	0	0	0	0	0
41	0	0	0	0	0	1	0	0	0	0	0
45	0	0	0	0	0	0	0	1	0	0	0
50	1	1	0	0	0	0	0	0	0	0	0
54	0	0	0	0	0	1	0	0	0	0	0
60	0	0	0	0	0	1	0	0	0	0	0
61	1	0	0	0	0	0	0	0	0	0	0
65	1	0	0	0	0	0	0	0	0	0	0
72	1	0	0	0	0	0	0	0	0	0	0
73	0	0	0	0	0	1	0	0	0	0	0
74	1	0	0	0	0	0	0	0	0	0	0
TOTALS	41	9	12	9	2	13	5	8	1	5	4

Key: pla = plain; bor = bored (centre); ma = marked (for centre-boring); cu + cut (centre); top-bor = hole bored on one edge (for suspension?)

TABLE 3: SHELL SQUARES, RECTANGLES AND TRIANGLES

Context	Squares	Rectangles					Triangles				
		Complete			Fragments						
		0p	2p	4p	1p	2p	pl	4npl	4n3p	1npl	frpl
None	0	0	0	1	0	0	0	0	0	0	0
2	0	0	0	0	0	0	0	0	1	0	0
3	1	0	0	0	0	2	1	2	1	1	0
6	1	0	0	0	0	0	0	0	0	0	0
7	0	2	0	0	0	0	0	0	0	0	0
9	0	0	0	0	0	0	0	1	0	0	0
11	0	0	0	0	0	0	1	0	0	0	0
12	0	3	0	3	0	0	0	1	0	0	0
14	0	1	0	0	0	0	0	0	0	0	0
16	0	1	0	0	0	0	0	0	0	0	0
22	0	1	0	0	0	0	0	0	0	0	0
23	0	1	0	0	0	0	0	0	0	0	0
24	0	0	0	0	0	0	0	0	1	0	1
27	0	0	0	0	0	0	1	0	0	0	0
29	0	1	0	0	0	0	0	0	0	0	0
40	0	1	0	1	0	1	0	0	0	0	0
43	0	1	0	0	0	0	0	0	0	0	0
50	0	0	0	1	0	0	0	0	0	0	0
57	0	0	1	0	0	0	0	0	0	0	0
59	0	0	0	0	0	0	1	0	0	0	0
74	0	0	0	0	1	0	0	0	0	0	1
TOTALS	2	12	1	6	1	3	4	4	3	1	2

Key: 0p = no perforations; 1, 2, 4p = 1, 2, 4 perforations; pl = plain; 4npl = 4 notched plain (no perfs); 4n3p = 4 notches 3 perforations; 1npl = 1 notch, plain; frpl = fragment, plain

There is some variation in the size range of the shell discs, particularly with the whole plain discs, with diameters ranging from around 15 mm to in excess of 50 mm. Thicknesses depend upon whether the outer portion of the valve has been removed or not. Where it has been removed, fine, well-finished discs may have a thickness of less than 2 mm, whereas a large disc still retaining the outer portion of the shell can have a thickness > 5 mm. In general, the smaller the disc, the better finished the artifact.

There is a considerable variation in the finished quality of these shell discs, ranging from crude angular 'rough outs', to those well-finished, with smoothly rounded sides, to those with the outer side of the valve removed, and those where it still remains. There is some evidence to suggest that well-finished discs were used for further working, i.e. for cutting out semi-circular holes, but there are also poorly finished discs, and half discs, which still retain the outer portion of the valve, and which have been only crudely shaped into a circular form. It seems likely that one purpose for shell discs was for cutting down into the shell crescents (see below). Heavy semi-circular centre-cut discs, usually of *Pinctada mazatlanica*, are regularly illustrated or referred to in the archaeological literatureas 'fishhooks' (e.g., Meggers, Evans and Estrada, 1965; Marcos and Norton, 1984; Mester, 1985, 1990). I do not feel wholly comfortable with this 'blanket' interpretation, however. Many of these artifacts are simply too fragile to have sustained this purpose, and there rarely seems any evidence of how they were secured to a line. For example, the copper fishhooks found at the site often retain evidence of a 'shank'. Some may indeed be fishhooks; others may have served different, possibly decorative functions, such as nose-rings for example, which seem to have been a common form of personal adornment worn by the coastal peoples in prehispanic times. Further, detailed analysis of this group is required to establish a more secure interpretation of their function.

Decorative Shell Plaques (Table 3)

These have been further classified under the sub-groups: 1) triangles, 2) rectangles, 3) squares and 4) spirals.

1) All triangles are manufactured from *P. mazatlanica*. This is another group of special artifacts for which a range of levels of working and degrees of finish can be demonstrated. Plain triangles, carefully cut out in the form of an equilateral triangle are found, there is one example with one notch cut out, others with four notches, and finally four notches with three small perforations, one at each point. It seems likely that the triangles served an ornamental purpose, either attached to clothing, or as necklace components.

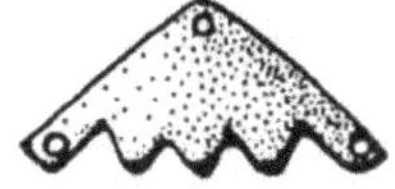

P. mazatlanica. Notched & Perforated Triangle (life-sized)

2) Rectangles are manufactured mainly from *P. mazatlanica*, although two were fashioned from *P. sterna*. As with the triangles, a range of levels of working and degrees of finish is demonstrable, with plain well-cut shell rectangles, to those with 2 (one at each end) or with 4 perforations (one at each corner). Again, it is likely that these were also for purposes of ornamentation, for attaching to clothing or as necklace components.

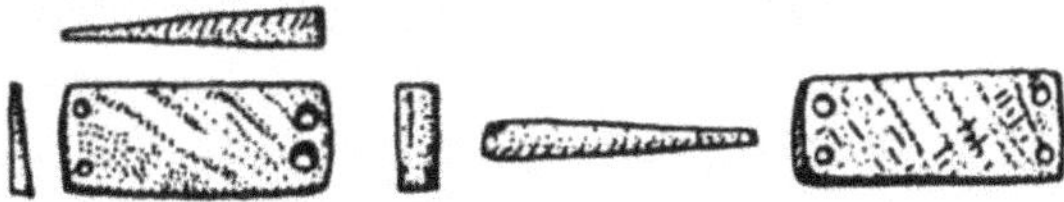

P. Mazatlanica. Perforated Rectangle (life-sized)

3) Only two finished squares were found, and they are ornately worked pieces, with two small perforations at two opposing corners, probably for attaching to clothing or incorporating into jewellery.

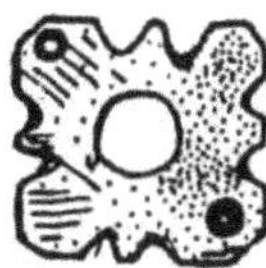

P. mazatlanica. Notched & Perforated Square (x 1.5 size)

4) Two 'finished' shell spirals were found, together with one piece of cut shell with concentric circular lines etched, presumably as a pattern for a spiral. They are manufactured from *P. mazatlanica*, and their purpose is unknown.

Shell Crescents (Table 4)

Shell crescents could otherwise be described as deliberately cut, or perhaps fractured, portions of shell rings except, as no whole shell rings were ever found, and very large numbers of the them are very fragmentary, it was felt presumptuous to assume a ring as their finished form. In reality, their final purpose is unknown. The great majority of the crescents were manufactured from the heavy pearl oyster shell, *P. mazatlanica*.

For analytical purposes, each crescent fragment was measured on a diameter chart, to allow calculation of the potential diameter were the circle complete, and also what portion of the circle remained. In this way, it could be seen that the majority were either of 20 mm diameter or of 50 mm diameter, and the average greatest remaining portions of the circle were calculated at around 18.75%. There are rare finds of crescents which are around 50% of a circle.

Likewise there is great variation in the relative thickness and width of the crescents, from < 2 mm wide and 1 mm thick up to > 4 mm wide and 2.5 mm thick. In general, this group seems to be too fragile to sustain more than an ornamental purpose. They are also sometimes referred to as 'fishhooks', but this cannot be correct (see Shell Discs above).

It is known that decorative nose rings and earrings were used during the Manteño period, and figurines with these ornaments are not uncommon. Given the general fragility of this group, it is not unlikely that a high level of fragmentation could be expected during manufacture. However it is hard to escape the conclusion that complete rings would have survived if that had been their intended final form. Possibly decorative 'hoops' were sewn into clothing, or otherwise incorporated as components of necklaces. Occasional ear or finger rings may also have been manufactured. Further analysis of this group may yield a better interpretation.

Shell Figures (Table 4)

Shell figures are almost exclusively manufactured from *P. mazatlanica*. A total of 18 shell figures were recovered during the course of the excavation. All are small and thin, between 20–30 mm long, and 3–5 mm thick. They are representations of marine animals: birds, fish and a seal. The boring of a small hole off–centre into four ofthese (see below) has been interpreted as evidence for their being components of atlatl equipment, as it is not clear how they could have been used as decorative pendant or necklace pieces. Other whole pieces of cut shell resemble 'rough out' stages for later working into a finished figure.

P. mazatlanica. Bored Bird Figure (half–size)

Spondylus. Bored Seal Figure (half–size)

Spondylus. Bored Bird Figure (half–size)

P. Mazatlanica. Fish Figure (half–size)

Cut Shell

A very large quantity of cut shell was recovered from many contexts in Trench A, the majority of which was not treated as 'special'. It was separated during the course of shell identification for further examination. However, some pieces which have been clearly prepared further for working into subsequent figures, ornaments etc have been included as special shell artifacts. Cut shell also includes fragmentary pieces, sometimes with one of more perforations, which it was impossible to classify further.

Shell Beads (Table 5)

This is a very large group of artifacts, with two principal sub–groups:

1) small beads fashioned from white shell (probably *Spondylus*) and red shell of the *Spondylus* species, and

2) beads of the species *Oliva undatella*.

1) Great diversity exists within this sub–group of shell beads, and further analysis of size variations is planned. Both white and spondylus beads range in size from around 2 mm in diameter to around 5 mm or slightly over, with the majority being around 4–5 mm, and about 1–2 mm thick. Around two thirds of both groups are perforated through the centre, but the remainder are 'blanks', that is, without perforations. There are also examples of beads fractured during the process of boring, or of 'errors' wherein they have been bored from both sides, but the drilled holes failed to meet. More detailed analysis of these beads should yield important information on the process of bead production here. Another sub–group consists of 'tubular' beads, beads whose length exceeds their diameter. These are usually of *Spondylus* sp., and once again there are a portion of these which are unbored 'blanks', or which show evidence of mistakes in the drilling process. Ethnohistoric sources refer to the value of strings of beads, known as *chaquira*, which had great value in trade (e.g., Cieza de León, 1864: 176).

2) Beads of the species *Oliva undatella* and (less commonly) *Olivella semistriata* differ greatly from the group described above. These are whole cylindrical shells which have had their spires removed to create a hole, possibly widened deliberately by passing a fine point through the opening. In this way, they may have been strung by attaching a thread through the aperture of the shell. *O. undatella* are very colourful, many being creamy white or pinkish red and cream striped, and would have been smooth and highly polished when new.

A second variation to this group are those which were cross–sectioned through the centre of the body whorl to remove the apex of the shell, and which have one perforation drilled near the base, giving the appearance of a fish's head.

Shell Tools

A total of 68 shell tools were found altogether. This final group of shell special artifacts differs from those described above, in that they were made from the columella of some medium– sized gastropod, probably the small conches *Strombus granulatus* and *S. gracilior*, presumably as tools. The whole artifact is 'handy', and has a sharpish point, many examples of which show signs of wear. Microscopic wear analysis should be carried out to see if it is possible to determine the likely use of these tools. However, it seems

TABLE 4: SHELL CRESCENTS, ORNAMENTS AND FIGURES									
CONTEXT	. . Crescents	Ornaments	Figures						
			brdpla	brdbor	objpla	zoopla	zoobor	antbor	fshpla
None	1	1	0	0	0	0	1	0	0
1	2	0	0	0	0	0	0	0	0
2	1	0	0	0	0	0	0	0	1
3	6	0	0	3	1	0	0	0	0
4	1	0	0	0	0	0	0	0	0
6	1	1	0	0	0	0	0	0	0
7	6	0	1	0	0	0	0	0	0
8	0	2	0	0	0	0	0	0	0
10	4	1	0	0	0	0	0	0	0
11	1	1	0	0	1	0	0	0	0
12	2	1	0	0	0	0	0	0	0
16	1	1	0	0	0	0	0	0	0
17	1	0	0	0	0	0	0	0	0
18	2	0	0	0	0	0	0	0	1
19	6	0	0	0	0	0	0	0	0
21	1	0	0	0	0	0	0	0	0
22	0	1	0	0	0	0	0	0	0
23	13	2	0	2	1	0	0	0	1
24	0	1	0	0	0	0	0	0	0
25	1	0	0	0	0	0	0	1	0
27	2	0	0	0	0	0	0	0	0
28	1	0	0	0	0	0	0	0	0
29	0	1	0	0	0	0	1	0	0
31	2	1	0	0	0	0	0	0	0
40	1	0	0	0	0	0	0	0	0
47	1	0	0	0	0	0	0	0	0
48	1	0	0	0	0	0	0	0	0
50	5	0	0	0	0	0	0	0	0
57	0	0	0	1	1	1	0	0	0
60	1	0	0	0	0	0	0	0	0
61	1	0	0	0	0	0	0	0	0
73	1	0	0	0	0	0	0	0	0
TOTAL	66	14	1	6	50	1	2	1	3

Key: Cresc = crescent; Orn = ornament; brdpla = bird plain (no bore); brdbor = bird bored; objpla = object plain; zoopla = zoomorphic plain; zoobor = zoomorphic bored; antbor = anthropomorphic bored; fshpla = fish plain

TABLE 5: SHELL BEADS							
Context	White Beads			Spondylus Beads			Oliva Beads
	Complete	Fragments	Tubular	Complete	Fragments	Tubular	
None	3	0	0	5	0	0	3
2	3	1	0	0	2	0	14
3	11	0	0	4	0	0	30
4	3	0	0	0	1	0	7
5	0	0	0	0	0	0	2
6	14	2	1	1	2	0	15
7	8	0	0	6	0	0	13
8	7	0	1	5	0	0	6
9	4	0	1	4	1	0	9
10	8	0	1	3	2	0	8
11	2	0	0	2	4	0	11
12	10	2	1	4	1	0	9
13	4	1	0	2	0	0	1
14	0	0	0	0	1	0	0
15	0	0	0	2	0	0	5
16	2	0	0	0	1	0	6
17	0	0	1	5	2	0	3
18	5	0	0	4	2	0	8
19	3	0	0	1	0	0	3
21	1	0	0	0	0	0	0
22	1	0	0	0	0	0	0
23	3	0	0	10	1	2	39
24	0	0	0	1	1	0	0
25	2	1	0	0	0	0	7
26	1	0	0	0	1	0	1
27	1	0	0	2	0	0	4
28	0	0	0	0	0	0	6
29	1	0	0	0	0	0	4
31	1	0	0	0	0	0	5
33	0	0	0	0	0	0	4
39	0	0	0	0	0	1	0
40	0	0	0	2	0	1	2
43	0	0	0	0	0	0	5
47	0	0	0	0	0	0	3
50	1	0	0	1	0	0	15
57	0	0	0	1	0	0	0
64	0	0	0	1	0	1	0
73	0	0	0	0	0	1	1
74	0	0	0	1	0	1	0
TOTALS	99	7	6	67	22	7	249

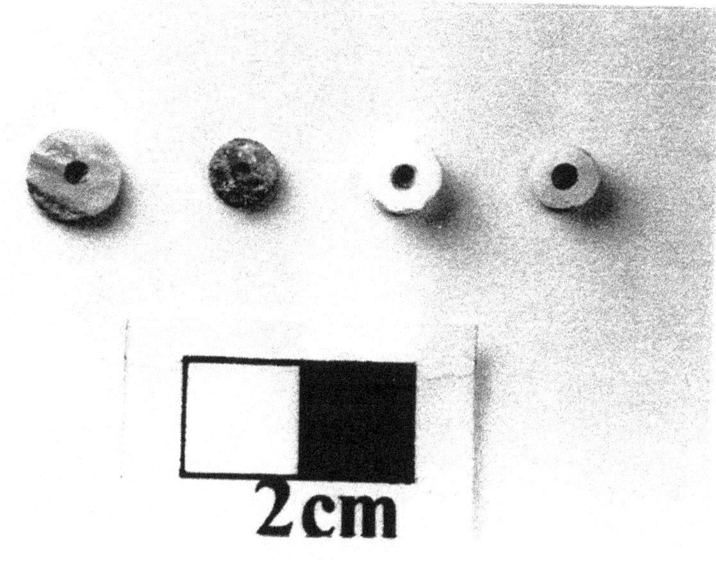

Spondylus beads

Oliva undatella 'fish head' beads

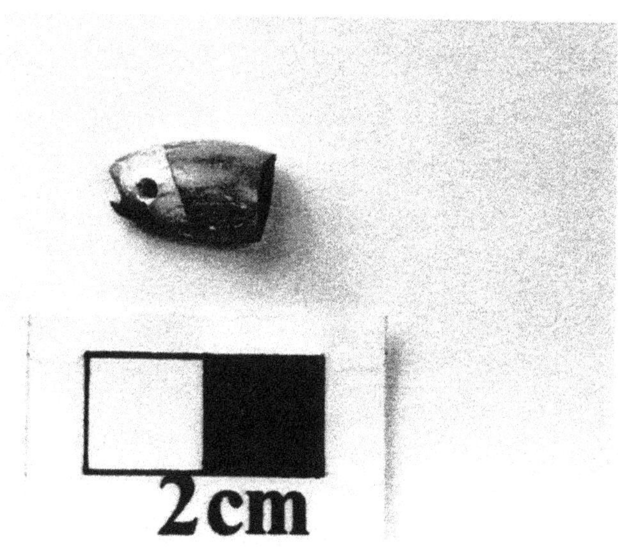

Oliva undatella 'fish head' beads

Copper needle/bodkins

quite possible that they were used as 'soft' instruments in the pressure–flaking or retouching of lithics in the prolific on-site chert–working industry here (see below).

CERAMIC ARTIFACTS (Table 6)

Ceramic special artifacts are similarly a very varied group and include figurines, discs and beads, described under separate headings below.

Figurines

Sixty seven figurines and parts of figurines were recovered in total from Trench A, with many of these clustering into the later, midden dump contexts. Figurines constitute probably the most important group of ceramic special artifacts and consist of artifacts of baked clay shaped into either human or animal form. Whilst there is a range of styles and sizes of figurines, most are around 40–50 mm in length, and many are fragments.

The single most prominent group are those of a very crude form, having a head with nose (usually fragmented), occasionally eye and mouth slits and no other features. They are of solid, plain baked clay, with no evidence of paint or slip. There is no complete example, but examination of different fragments confirms an overall primitive impression - of crudely made legs and arms with few details. This style of figurine is purportedly typical of late Guangala, transition to early Manteño (Eric López, personal communication), but more analysis must be carried out to confirm this. Three other important figurine finds should be mentioned, in that they help to date the contexts in which they were found.

The first is a solid head fragment (possibly a vessel adorno) of what looks to be a vampire bat, made of dark grey reduce–fired clay, deriving from a late context #12. The second is a fine, complete example of hollow polished blackware deriving from the earliest 'late' context #23. It depicts a seated individual with an elongated headdress, possibly indicative of head deformation. He has what seem to be earspools and is ornately decorated with incised spirals. Several holes, including a large one in the back, pierce the fabric, and may be for whistling purposes. This figurine is almost certainly of the Manteño period.

The third, nicknamed 'Bart Simpson', deriving from context #72, is very different in style from any of the others. It is a solid fragment of the head portion of a human form, with stylised hair/headdress, 'coffee bean' eyes and prominent hooked nose. There is no evidence of surface treatment such as slip or paint, and as yet it has not been possible to ascertain the period or culture of this style. However, with the hair incisions and the coffee bean eyes, the style is clearly quite earlier than Manteño. Solid figurines with coffee bean eyes and hooked noses occur from Middle Formative Machalilla times, and continue down into the early Regional Developmental Period. This figurine fragment could therefore be late Engoroy, early Guangala, or possibly Bahía.

Although hollow figurines are the most common type from Late Formative Chorrera–Engoroy times onwards into the Manteño culture, and the majority of figurine finds from sites in coastal Ecuador are of the hollow sort, there are only occasional very fragmented examples from Trench A of the Midden site. Most of the figurine finds are solid, and fairly crudely made. Questions raised by factors such as these will be looked at further in the ceramic section in the Second Report to follow.

Ceramic Discs

Ceramic discs constitute the next most important group of ceramic special finds after the figurines. They are manufactured from pottery fragments, possibly broken pot sherds, although interestingly, very few ceramic discs display any curvature, which implies they were made either from the body sherds of very large vessels, from neck sherds, or were specially manufactured. The majority of them are of polished blackware on one side only, and often bear burnished line decoration. A few were manufactured from red slipped pottery, although this is not common.

They exactly parallel shell discs in terms of their range of size, thickness, method of treatment and finish. There are those, usually small, with diameters of around 20 mm and thicknesses of around 3 mm which are smoothly rounded and well- finished. Larger examples (the largest is 60 by 50 mm and 7 mm thick) are often more crudely made and less well–finished. Some are plain, others are marked in the centre, presumably prior to boring, some have small neat perforations through the centre, and still others have been cut in two, and then have large semi- circular cuts out of the centre, just like their shell counterparts.

It is difficult to imagine what these discs may have been used for. Some may have been used as crude spindle whorls; others possibly as small net–weights, to facilitate even casting of an open net. Whereas shell discs may well have been made, then used or traded as handy–sized raw material for the later production of a variety of mother–of–pearl ornaments, it is hard to see the ceramic discs serving a similar purpose, although they parallel the shell discs very closely in all other respects. One may also speculate that they were used either as game counters, or possibly as tokens in exchange.

Spindle Whorls

Spindle whorls constitute another group of ceramic special artifacts. Altogether, fifteen were found, two of which are fragments. Apart from one redware example, the others are of blackware, with incised geometric designs (see e.g., Lathrap, 1975: 107 plates 538–540; 543–549).

Ceramic Seals

Twenty one ceramic seals were found from Trench A, many of these in small fragments. There seems to be a slight association between the earlier contexts and the location of these seals (Table 6). All but one are 'flat' stamps with

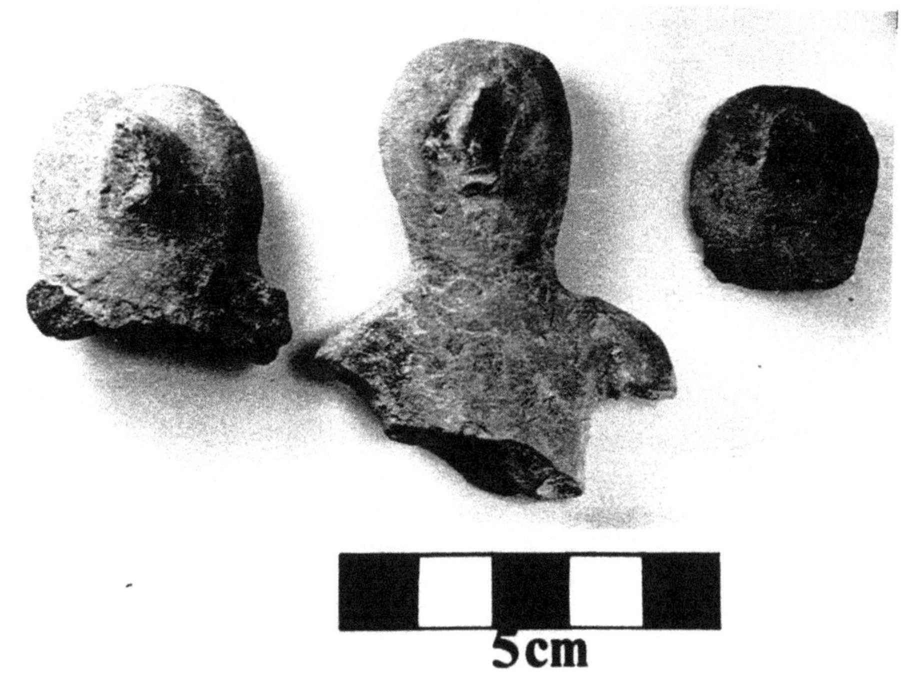

Fragments of solid figurines

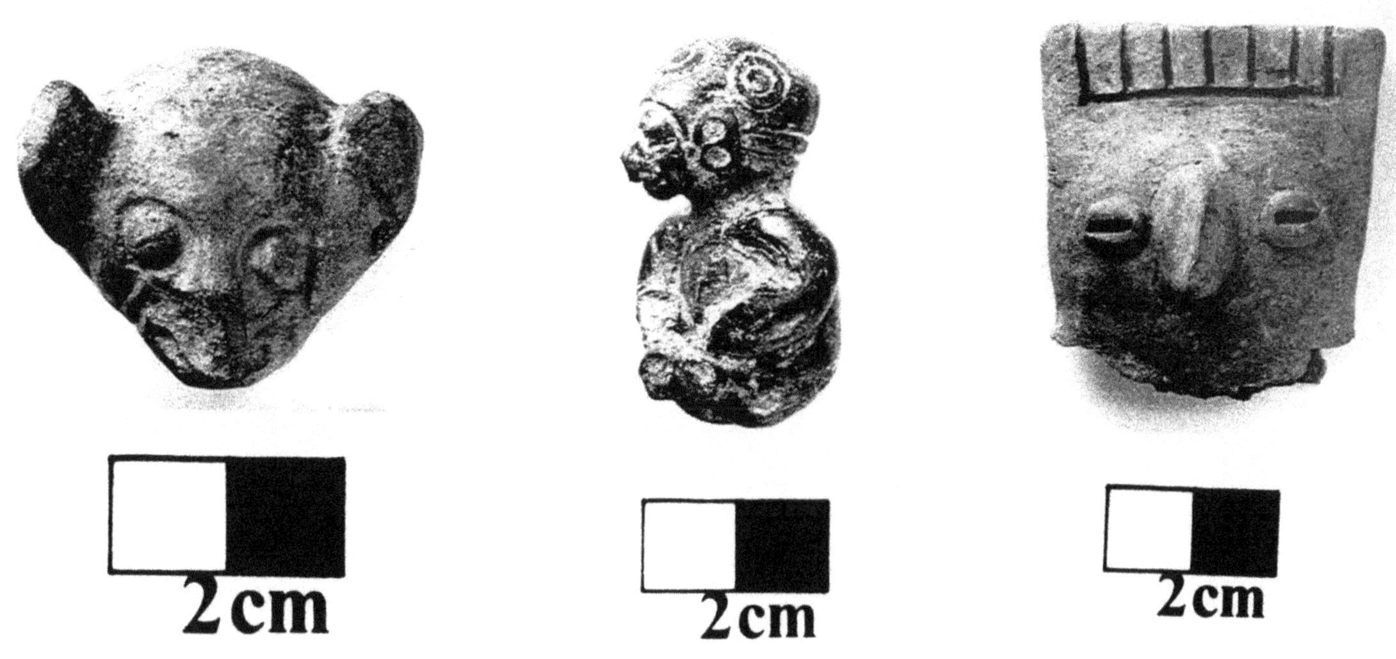

Vampire bat head of figurine or adorno

Incised black Manteño ocarina (whistle)

'Bart Simpson' solid figurine head

TABLE 6: CERAMIC ARTEFACTS

Context	Disc	Figurine	Vessel	Spindle	Seal	Spoon	Sherd	1SegB ead	2SegB ead	3SegB ead	4SegB ead	5SegB ead	6SegB ead	7/+SegB ead
None	3	1	0	0	1	0	1	1	0	0	4	2	2	2
2	1	3	0	1	0	1	0	0	0	0	0	0	0	0
3	7	6	0	3	0	1	0	1	1	0	1	0	3	0
4	2	0	0	0	0	0	0	0	0	0	1	1	1	0
5	0	1	0	0	0	0	0	0	0	0	0	0	0	0
6	4	8	0	0	0	1	0	0	2	1	4	1	0	2
7	3	2	0	1	0	1	0	0	1	0	0	1	1	0
9	2	0	0	1	0	1	0	1	3	0	1	0	0	0
10	2	2	1	2	0	0	1	0	0	1	3	0	2	0
11	3	2	0	1	0	0	0	0	2	1	0	1	0	2
12	1	2	0	0	0	0	0	0	1	0	0	0	0	2
13	1	1	0	0	0	0	0	0	0	1	2	0	0	0
15	1	0	0	0	0	0	0	0	1	0	0	1	1	0
16	1	1	0	0	0	0	0	0	2	1	0	1	0	0
17	0	0	0	0	0	1	0	0	0	1	0	0	0	0
18	0	2	0	0	0	0	0	0	1	2	0	3	0	1
19	4	2	0	1	1	2	1	0	0	0	0	1	1	1
21	2	0	0	0	0	0	0	0	0	1	0	0	0	0
22	0	0	0	0	0	0	0	0	0	1	0	0	0	0
23	3	15	0	2	3	3	1	2	16	33	11	5	1	1
24	0	0	0	0	0	0	0	0	0	1	0	0	1	0
25	2	0	0	0	0	0	0	0	0	4	0	0	0	0
26	0	1	0	0	1	0	0	0	0	0	0	0	0	0
27	2	2	0	0	1	0	0	0	2	3	1	2	0	0

Context	Disc	Figurine	Vessel	Spindle	Seal	Spoon	Sherd	1SegBead	2SegBead	3SegBead	4SegBead	5SegBead	6SegBead	7/+SegBead
28	1	0	0	0	1	0	0	0	0	1	1	0	0	2
29	1	2	0	0	0	0	0	0	0	3	1	3	1	0
30	1	0	0	0	0	0	0	0	0	0	0	0	0	0
31	1	1	0	0	0	0	0	0	0	0	1	0	0	0
36	1	0	0	0	0	0	0	0	0	1	1	0	0	0
39	0	0	0	0	0	0	0	0	0	1	1	0	0	0
40	0	0	0	0	0	0	0	0	0	1	0	0	1	0
43	0	0	0	1	0	0	0	0	0	2	0	1	3	2
47	0	0	0	0	0	0	0	0	0	0	0	0	0	1
48	1	0	0	0	0	0	0	0	0	0	0	0	0	0
50	3	0	1	0	2	1	0	0	0	1	0	0	0	0
54	0	1	0	0	0	0	0	0	0	0	0	0	0	0
57	0	1	0	1	1	3	0	0	0	1	0	0	0	1
58	0	1	0	0	1	0	0	0	0	0	0	0	0	0
61	0	1	0	0	0	1	0	0	0	0	0	0	0	0
62	1	0	0	0	0	0	0	0	0	0	0	0	0	0
64	0	0	1	1	0	0	0	0	0	0	0	0	0	0
65	0	2	1	0	1	0	0	0	0	0	0	0	0	0
70	0	0	0	0	0	1	0	0	0	0	0	0	0	0
72	0	1	0	0	1	1	0	0	0	0	0	0	0	0
73	2	2	1	0	4	0	0	0	0	0	0	0	0	0
74	0	2	0	0	3	0	2	0	0	0	0	0	0	0
93	0	2	0	0	0	0	1	0	0	0	0	0	0	0
TOTAL	56	67	5	15	21	18	7	5	32	62	33	23	18	17

Key: Most of the categories above are self-explanatory.
Vessel = decorated/modelled vessels or small whole vessels;
Sherds = eg textile impressed; 1 - 6 Seg Beads = segmented tubular beads

Ceramic discs

Spindle whorls

Ceramic seals

longated handles, and bear a variety of designs which ncorporate linear, spiral and stepped fret motifs. There is ne very fragmentary example of a cylinder seal. Ceramic eals are very common from Formative period Chorrera ulture onward (see e.g., Lathrap, 1975: 106 plates 515–37).

Segmented Tubular Beads

egmented tubular beads form another very distinctive roup. At first it was difficult to form an impression of the urpose of these artifacts. They are long narrow ceramic ıbes, between 5 and 20 mm long and 2–3 mm diameter, onsisting of, on average, 5 or 6 bead shaped segments, and ave a central perforation which would allow them to be trung. They seem to be made of a very hard ceramic aterial, and range in colour from black, grey, red to brown, lthough the great majority are black. Fragmentary xamples consisting of one to three or four segments are ommon, and occasionally examples with up to ten segments ave been found, but the majority have five or six.

able 6 shows an interesting tendency for finds of these eads to be concentrated together into certain contexts (e.g., s 6, 10, 11, 16, 18, 23, 27, 29 and 43), particularly the three six segment beads, which suggests a number of ossibilities: that the beads were manufactured 'long' and agmented as they fell, or were discarded by the artisan if ey broke, or that they formed parts of composite items of dornment (i.e., necklace), which fell into one area. It seems ost likely that these artifacts were manufactured with the ırpose of incorporating into a necklace or for another ecorative purpose.

Vessels

small group of ceramic special artifacts are whole vessels r fragmentary examples), such as tiny whole bowls, or arts of vessels bearing elaborate decorative moulded motif, ich as Manteño blackware jars with a face design upon the urviving neck portion. These will be described in greater etail in the ceramic report to follow.

Ceramic Spoons

final important group are the ceramic ladles or spoons, of hich eighteen were found. These are shallow, dish shaped tifacts which have one of two basic handle types: long, with e end in the form of a hand, or short, plain and pointed.

BONE ARTIFACTS

e next major group of finds are the items fashioned from ne. There are tools, such as bone points, but the most gnificant group are the polished cut bone segments, which ost likely served a decorative purpose, probably as cklace components. Identification of species has yet to be rried out, though it is thought that the majority of these ne artifacts are fashioned from the humeruses of bird ecies (Patrick Gay, 1993: personal communication). During the course of the excavations, many cut articulating ends of the humeruses of bird bones were found.

Bone Segments (Table 7)

TABLE 7: BONE SEGMENTS			
Context	Segments	Context	Segments
None	3	19	12
2	7	21	2
3	38	22	1
4	6	23	15
5	1	24	1
6	12	25	13
7	18	27	9
8	8	29	17
9	2	31	1
10	26	39	1
11	9	43	6
12	14	45	2
13	3	50	5
15	1	57	1
16	3	70	1
17	3	73	3
18	3	74	3
TOTAL	157	GRAND TOTAL	250

Altogether 250 bone segments were found during the excavation of Trench A. Readers will note clustering of the segments, particularly into the later contexts such as #s 3, 6, 7, 10, 12, 19, 23 and 29, which are interpreted as being mainly from the later midden dump. There is a great range in the size of these segments, from less than 10 mm long and around 2 mm wide, to over 40 mm long and 10 mm wide. Most commonly however, there are three size groups: around 15 mm long and 7 mm wide, 30 mm long by 7 mm wide, and 20 mm long and 8 mm wide. Many of the segments are flat, but some have a nearly circular or triangular cross–section. It is not uncommon for the segments to retain cut marks at one or both ends, and clearly many of them have been deliberately well–polished. Three rare examples have been decorated with horizontal lines grooved at either end. It seems probable that they were used decoratively, as components for items of jewellery, such as collars and bracelets.

Points

No true bone needles were found, such as exist in copper, with proper 'eyes', but five bone points were found. Apart from two examples which are clearly fragmented and may therefore once have possessed an 'eye' end, the others have one pointed end and one blunted, two of these with a deliberately worked 'spatula' end. The longest needle is 75 mm long by 3 mm wide, and the shortest 46 mm by 4 mm at the broad end. The points appear still to be well–pointed and little worn. It is difficult to offer an acceptable interpretation for their use; possibly for making holes in leather garments which have not survived, or for use in weaving or basketry (see e.g., Lathrap, 1975: 105 plates 495–500).

Bone Musical Instruments

One fragment of a bone whistle or pipe was found from context #73 at Trench A. It is 42 mm long and has three complete perforations along the shaft, and one fragmentary perforation. More whistle fragments were found from Trench B, to be reported in the Second Report to follow. Bone and ceramic flutes and whistles have a long tradition in Ecuador (again, see e.g., Lathrap, 1975: 105 plates 501–504; Mester, 1990: 142).

COPPER ARTIFACTS (Table 8)

There are five main categories of copper artifact: pins and needles, tools, bells, fishhooks and miscellaneous fragments of copper wire. The condition of the copper artifacts varies greatly, from well–preserved, to badly corroded and in need of expert conservation treatment.

TABLE 8: COPPER ARTEFACTS

Context	Needle	Pin	Hook	Ring	Tool	Bell	Tweezer
None	2	0	1	0	0	0	0
3	0	0	0	1	0	0	0
4	0	1	1	0	0	0	0
5	0	0	0	0	0	1	0
6	0	0	1	0	0	0	0
7	1	0	0	0	1	1	0
9	0	0	1	0	0	1	0
10	0	0	0	0	2	0	0
15	0	0	0	0	0	0	1
19	0	1	0	0	0	0	0
22	0	1	0	0	0	0	0
23	0	1	1	1	1	0	0
24	0	0	0	1	0	0	0
25	0	0	0	0	0	1	0
27	1	0	0	0	0	0	0
28	0	0	0	1	0	0	0
29	0	0	1	0	0	0	0
57	1	0	0	0	1	0	0
59	0	0	0	1	1	0	0
69	1	0	0	0	0	0	0
73	0	0	1	0	0	0	0
93	1	0	0	0	0	0	0
Totals	7	4	7	5	6	4	1

Ceramic spoon

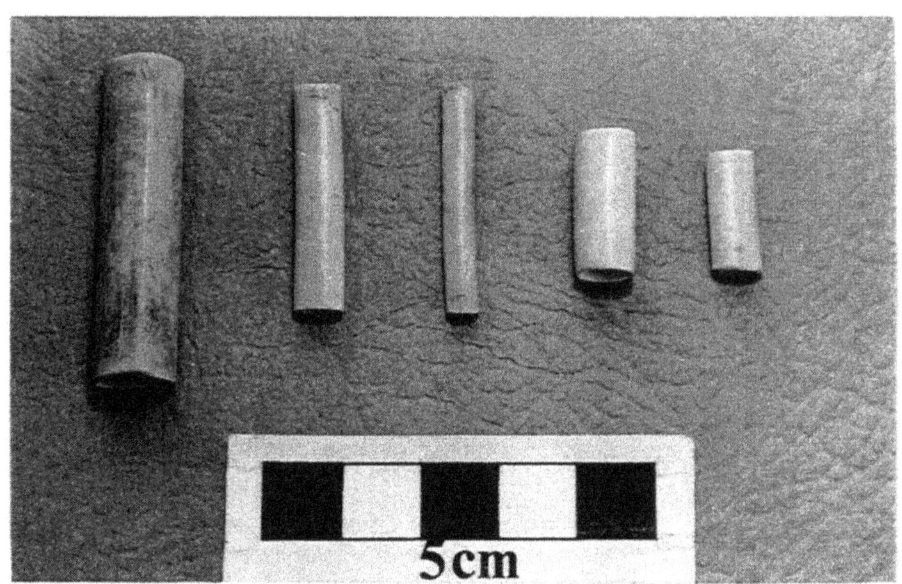

Bone segments

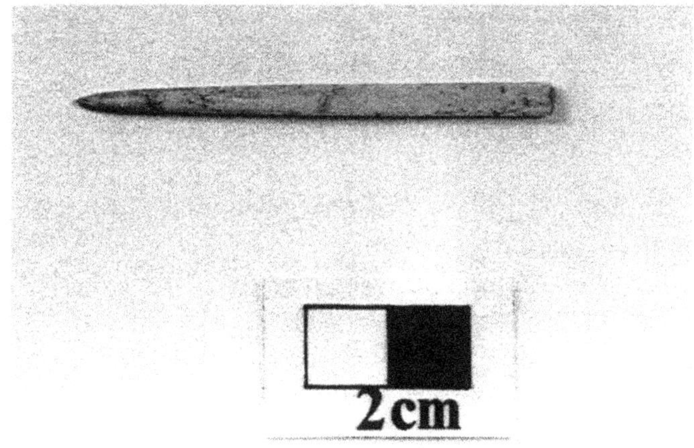

Bone point

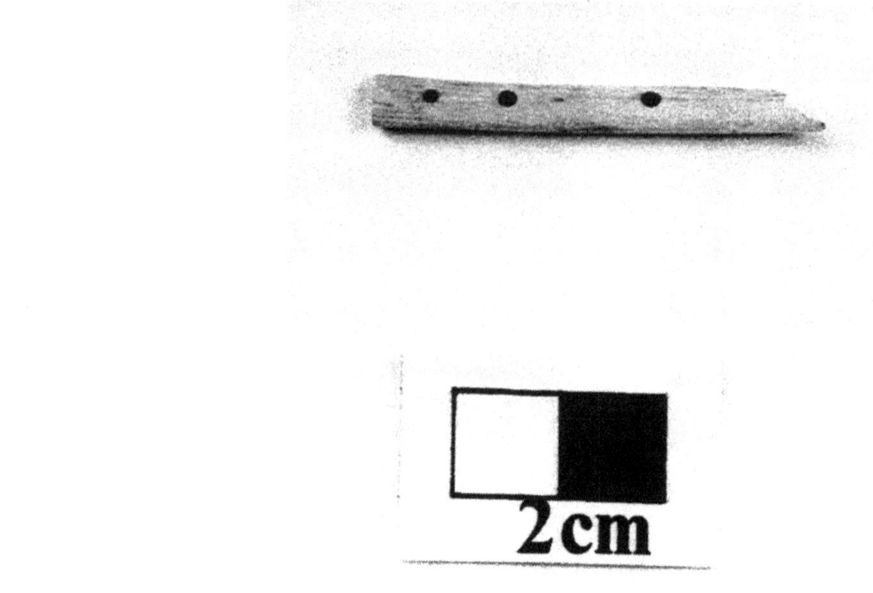

Bone whistle

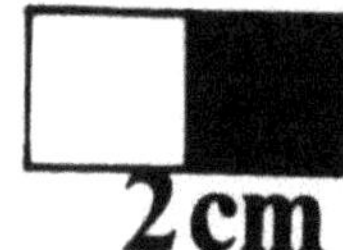

Copper needle/bodkins

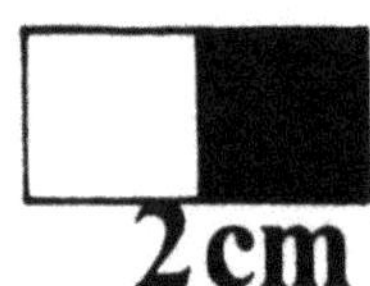

Copper bells: 'cascabeles'

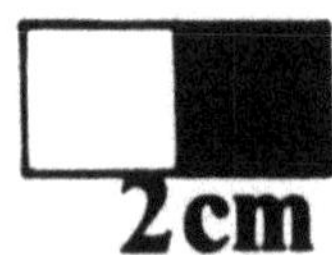

Copper fishhooks

Pins and Needles

There are more copper pins and needles than their bone counterparts. Apart from one fine pin with a point at either end, the other artifacts are clearly needles, with complete eyes, or eye remains. The longest, rather misshapen example, is nearly 140 mm long and 2 mm diameter at the intact eye end. The point is still 'good'. The pin is 75 mm long, and has a square cross– section 2 mm at its widest. Another complete needle is 80 mm long and 25 mm diameter. They were probably one aspect of the on–site production of finished decorative goods, whether items of jewellery of decorated clothing.

Tools

This group of six artifacts are about 30 mm long by 7 mm wide, are crudely pointed at one end, and may have been hafted to serve the purpose of, for example, a drill. Microscopic wear analysis may clarify further the purpose of these artifacts.

Bells

Four small bells were discovered from the later, upper contexts of Trench A. They are about 6–7 mm long by 5 mm wide, and still retain their 'ringing' element. Each has two small perforations at the rear, which suggests they may have been attached to clothing. Bells are mentioned in the account of the voyage of Bartolomeo Ruiz in 1525 (see section 8.2 below).

Fishhooks

Five copper fishhooks were found, three of which retain their shank ends for attaching to a line.

Miscellaneous

Diverse pieces of corroded copper wire were found, probably used in the manufacture of copper items; also fragments of what were probably copper finger rings, including one whole, bent example. The best example of a single–item copper artifact was a pair of tweezers, probably used either for depilatory purposes, or for the sorting or handling of fine or delicate artifacts or components in the production of decorative or luxury items in this area.

LITHIC ARTIFACTS (Table 9)

The final group of special artifacts is the lithic group, comprising microlithic and macrolithic artifacts. Chert is the dominant material in the lithic industry, with very large numbers of blades, flakes, cores and debitage being found, evidence of an important on–site industry here, further supported by the finding of lithic working artifacts such as a cut deer antler, most probably used in the 'soft' flaking of chert and obsidian blades.

The single most important group of chert tools are the small chert drills, of which 241 in total were found during the course of the excavations in Trench A. Obsidian flakes and blades were also found, including fine knives and scrapers, and also large stone artifacts briefly described under the macrolithics sub– heading. The lithic artifacts have been subject to a separate study which will be dealt with as a separate specialist report, to be included in the Second Report. Because of this, the different categories referred to below are described briefly.

Chert Drills

Two hundred and forty one chert drills were found during the course of the excavation of Trench A, and readers will note from Table 9 that many of these are concentrated into the later contexts, particularly #s 3, 6, 12, 16 and 23. There is much variation within this class of artifact, in degrees of finish and in of manner of use and fracture, as well as in size. Also, a range of different coloured cherts was used, and individual drills may be white, yellow, brown, black or a mixture of colours. The great majority are around 20 mm long and 6 mm wide, with tiny elongated hafting ends, and points for drilling. Very small examples of around 14 mm long and 3 mm wide exist, and likewise larger forms of around 30 mm long and 5 mm wide. These latter are rarely as well finished as the smaller forms. Four rarer, longer types were found, having elongated points at either end and measuring around 45 mm long and 6 mm wide. The best examples have much finely worked retouching.

Obsidian Tools

A number of fine obsidian flakes, blades and scrapers were found during the excavations at Trench A, underlining contact and trade between the sierra and the coast at this time. Table 9 shows a fairly random distribution of the 60 obsidian artifacts throughout contexts. The specialist lithics report will describe the different tool types in more detail.

Other Tools

A range of other chert tools, including large worked points, scrapers, blades and flakes were found. Some of these appear in Table: 9. However, the specialist lithics analysis will probably discover other tools within the generalised lithics material, so that the numbers of ordinary unretouched blades, flakes and scrapers may well increase. These will be described in the report to follow.

Macrolithics

Other than the chert and obsidian industry, large stone artifacts were found during the course of the excavations, probably of volcanic material. This macrolithic group include several stone netweights, fragments of elongated bar–shaped manos, hammerstones, metate fragments and one large flat stone slab, fashioned into the likeness of a fish, found in context #19.

TABLE 9: LITHIC ARTEFACTS									
Context	Chert				Obsidian	Macrolithics			
	Dr	Bl	Tl	Ot		Ax	Ma	Nw	Ha
None	6	0	0	0	1	0	0	0	0
1	2	0	0	0	0	0	0	0	0
2	3	0	4	0	4	0	0	0	0
3	41	3	1	0	5	1	0	1	1
4	2	1	0	0	1	0	0	0	0
5	2	0	0	0	0	0	0	0	0
6	22	0	0	2	0	0	0	1	0
7	3	1	1	0	0	0	0	0	0
8	2	0	1	0	0	0	0	0	0
9	8	0	0	0	2	0	0	0	0
10	8	0	0	0	0	0	0	1	0
11	4	1	2	0	1	0	0	0	0
12	21	0	0	0	1	0	0	0	0
13	7	0	0	0	0	0	0	0	0
14	0	0	1	0	0	0	0	0	0
15	2	0	0	0	0	0	0	0	0
16	11	0	1	0	1	0	0	0	0
18	5	2	1	0	1	0	0	0	0
19	8	0	0	0	2	0	2	4	0
21	3	0	0	0	0	0	0	0	0
22	1	0	0	0	0	0	0	0	0
23	28	0	2	0	16	0	3	5	1
24	0	0	0	0	3	0	0	0	0
25	2	1	1	0	1	0	0	0	0
27	2	0	0	0	2	0	1	1	0
28	0	0	0	0	2	0	0	0	0
29	2	0	0	0	0	0	0	0	0
33	4	0	0	0	1	0	0	0	0
39	2	0	0	0	1	0	3	0	2
40	3	0	0	0	1	0	0	1	0
43	1	0	0	0	2	0	0	0	0
47	2	0	0	0	0	0	1	1	0
48	0	0	0	0	1	0	0	0	0
50	9	0	0	0	0	0	1	0	0
54	1	0	0	0	1	0	0	0	0

TABLE 9: LITHIC ARTEFACTS									
Context	Chert				Obsidian	Macrolithics			
	Dr	Bl	Tl	Ot		Ax	Ma	Nw	Ha
56	1	0	0	0	1	0	0	0	0
57	7	0	0	0	1	0	0	0	0
59	2	0	0	0	0	0	0	1	0
60	3	0	0	0	0	0	0	0	0
61	2	0	0	0	2	0	1	1	0
62	1	0	0	0	0	0	0	0	0
64	1	0	0	0	0	0	1	0	0
69	0	0	0	0	1	0	0	0	0
72	2	0	0	0	2	0	0	0	0
73	0	0	0	0	1	0	0	0	0
74	4	0	0	0	3	0	0	0	0
93	1	0	0	0	0	0	0	0	0
94	0	0	0	0	0	0	0	1	0
TOTALS	241	9	15	2	60	2	13	19	4

Key: Dr = drill; Bl = blade; Tl = tool; Obsid = obsidian;
Ax = axe; Ma = mano; Nw = net-weight; Ha = hammerstone

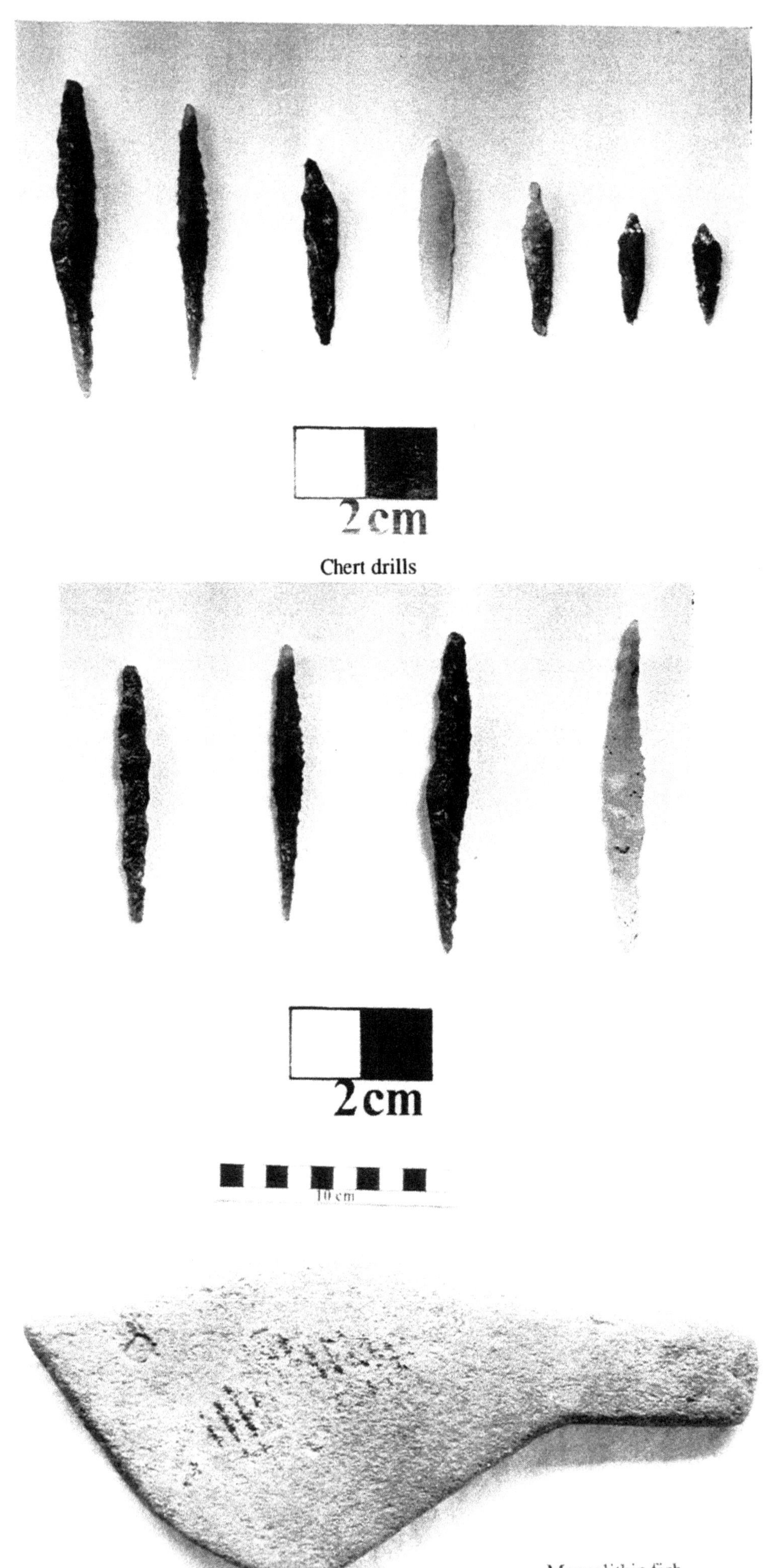

Chert drills

Macrolithic fish

OBSERVATIONS ON THE POTTERY FROM TRENCH A

As mentioned in the introduction above, preliminary observation of the pottery suggests the early Manteño period, with some earlier Guangala and Engoroy styles and forms. In particular, a pronounced shift in pottery types, from highly polished Manteño style blackware of the upper contexts, to polished red painted pottery in forms typical of the Engoroy period, particularly from the floor context #72, suggest at least a dual phase of occupation at this site. Many coarse–ware graters are present from the middle and later phase contexts, in far greater proportion to the rarer finds of 'quality' wares.

CHAPTER 4

ANALYSIS OF FAUNAL MATERIALS

(by Kathleen E. Clark)

Introduction

A large and diverse quantity of faunal material was recovered from site OMJPLP15. The analysis of this material will be a lengthy process. The remains have been divided into six fractions for separate processing: 1) vertebrates, 2) mollusca, 3) echinoderms, 4) corals, 5) cirripedia (barnacles), and 6) decapod crustaceans. Preliminary analyses of the vertebrate and molluscan fractions have begun, the corals and barnacles have been weighed (contexts 1 to 27) but not yet identified, and the echinoderms and decapod crustacean materials remain unanalyzed because the process of separating them from the shell and bone fractions is still incomplete. All faunal remains have been saved for future more-detailed analysis and as voucher specimens.

Mollusca

Shell material from OMJPLP15 was separated into two categories: 1) **shell specials** (tools, beads, disks, plaques, etc. and their recognizable precursors) and 2) **raw shell** material. The shell specials were removed prior to the processing of the raw shell, thus these items were not included in the species counts or weights determined for each unit and context. Shell weights will have been only negligibly reduced by the removal of the shell specials. Likewise, the species counts will have been little affected except in the case of *Oliva undatella*, a species represented by very few unmodified individuals.

The **raw shell** was further divided into two subcategories: 1) cut shell (essentially a group of 'sub-specials' which includes fragments with cut edges and shells bearing the characteristic marks of damage during opening for the removal of meat) and 2) shells with no macroscopic evidence of human modification (most shell material is in this group).

The analysis of the raw shell from OMJPLP15 has not yet been completed. To date, a preliminary analysis has been accomplished for the 77 units of contexts 1 to 27. This represents about half of the shell material recovered from the excavation. For these units, the following procedures were undertaken:

1) Any specials, non-molluscan remains, and unidentifiable calcined material were removed for separate analysis. The origin of the calcined material (shell, coral, bone?) could not be definitely determined, but this material is presumed to be the result of lime manufacture. It was weighed separately.

2) All shells and shell fragments were separated by taxonomic unit (usually species; otherwise, genus or family). Taxonomic identifications were based on the standard malacological reference works for the Panamic Faunal Province (Olsson 1961 and Keen 1971), taking the nomenclature employed by Keen.

3) Any remaining unidentifiable shell fragments were divided into two categories: nacreous and non-nacreous. This separation was made because the López Viejo Site was a mother-of- pearl workshop, thus the nacreous fragments, although unidentifiable, represent part of the raw material for the manufacture of beads, disks, plaques, etc.

4) The number of valves was counted for each taxonomic unit. Fragments were counted as separate valves when they confidently could be identified as distinct individuals. In the case of pelecypods, left and right valves were separately enumerated.

5) The minimum number of individuals (MNI) was determined for each taxonomic unit. For gastropods and scaphopods, the number of identified valves (whole or fragmentary) was taken as MNI. For polyplacophorans, MNI was calculated as the number of valves divided by eight. Where possible, the right and left valves of pelecypod taxa were paired for the determination of MNI, but for those taxa (especially the pearl oysters *Pteria sterna* and *Pinctada mazatlanica*) in which entire valves were uncommon, MNI was taken as the greater number of either right or left valves.

6) For each taxonomic unit, cut shell pieces were separated and counted. The cut shell subcategory pertains almost exclusively to the two pearl oyster species; other taxa rarely included cut pieces. The number of burned individuals or fragments was also noted.

7) The shell material was weighed in the following fractions: a) total shell (excluding only specials and unidentified calcined material), b) total fragments (all unidentified shell fragments), c) nacreous fragments, d) total *P. sterna* (including cut pieces), e) total *P. mazatlanica*, f) total *Spondylus princeps*, g) total *Spondylus calcifer*, h) total unidentifiable *Spondylus*, i) total cut shell for each of the above and any other relevant taxa.

8) Barnacles and corals were weighed as part of the shell analysis procedure. No attempt was made to calculate the MNI of barnacles as these were mostly present as shattered fragments. Minimum number of individuals is a meaningless concept for corals; these were counted as number of chunks. The barnacles and corals have not yet been identified; several species of each are present in the collections from the López Viejo Site.

9) The raw data from each unit were entered into a data base system.

The total MNI found in the 77 units of contexts 1-27 was

30,160. Gastropods account for 88.16% of the total; bivalves, 7.48%; and others (scaphopods and polyplacophorans), 4.35%. A list of the molluscan taxa tentatively identified to date from OMJPLP15 is included as Appendix A; it includes 64 bivalves, 95 gastropods, 1 scaphopod, and 1 polyplacophoran. The analysis of the remaining excavation contexts will almost certainly augment this list and it is hoped that a more careful examination of certain groups will resolve some taxonomic ambiguities.

The number of molluscan species identified from the López Viejo site is extraordinary, greatly exceeding the numbers reported from any other Ecuadorian archaeological site, including the nearby Manteño shell working sites at Salango (OMJPLP140) and Los Frailes (OMJPMH108F), or a composite list from 223 sites in El Oro Province. Allan (n.d.) reported a total of 57 shellfish taxa from the excavations at site OMJPLP140, Mester (1990) identified 86 taxa from OMJPMH108F, while Clark and Netherly (1990) found a minimum of 63 species in El Oro. While it is difficult to evaluate the shell identification and counting procedures employed by Mester and (especially) by Allan, it is unlikely that prodedural differences can account entirely for the great discrepancy in species richness. The López Viejo site may well contain more molluscan species than any other archaeological site reported worldwide.

In terms of molluscan species diversity, López Viejo is also an unusual site. The diversity index we have employed is the Shannon–Weaver Index (H'), the measure most commonly used in biological and ecological investigations[1]. This index includes a component of species richness (the number of species) and a component of percent abundance (evenness of distribution), thus it gives an indication of the tendency to focus the shell gathering effort on just a few species or to spread that effort over many species (higher values indicating greater diversity).

It should be understood that the difficulties inherent in the counting and identification of archaeological shell material result in some lack of precision in the calculation of species diversity. Some of the taxonomic units assigned (genus, family) may include two or more species. Moreover, the taxonomic units are not always mutually exclusive. For example, we have identified four species of *Columbella* at OMJPLP15, but there are many fragmentary individuals that can be assigned to the genus *Columbella* but not to any particular species. This generic level identification represents some mixture of the four identified species and perhaps others as well. In calculating species diversity for the López Viejo site, we have included only those taxonomic units we believe to be unique species. The exclusion of ill-defined or confounded taxa (e.g., *Columbella* sp.) eliminated about 6% of the total MNI. The net impact of the exclusion was almost certainly to lower the calculated diversity. An additional and insurmountable problem is the possibility that some individuals have been counted more than once. This can occur if parts of the shell (e.g., the left and right valves of pelecypods) are recovered in different units.

The calculated values of H' for each unit of contexts 1 to 27 at OMJPLP15 range from 1.03 to 3.20, and the overall diversity of the 77 units combined is 2.45. Context 23, which contained a very large quantity of shell and was heavily dominated by the small gastropod *Olivella semistriata*, stands out as relatively undiverse (H'=1.32); this context pulls down the overall site diversity. By comparison, we have computed the diversity of molluscan taxa for 11 contexts at the Los Frailes Site (OMJPMH– 108F) using Mester's (1990) data; H' for these samples ranges from 0.60 to 1.76, with an overall value of 0.98. In El Oro, shell diversity values for 17 sites were reported by Clark and Netherly (1990) and ranged from 0.03 to 1.48. The data reported by Allan (n.d.) for the Salango shell working site (OMJPLP140) unfortunately do not permit the calculation of species diversity.

Compared to these other sites, López Viejo exhibits a very diversified shellfish gathering effort. The high diversity values reflect both the large number of species exploited and the evenness of their distribution. Only 15 out of 161 species had abundance values greater than 1%, and only three species, *Olivella semistriata*, *Fissurella* sp. #1, and *Tegula panamensis*, exceeded 5% of the total MNI. In contrast, the Los Frailes site was dominated by *Cerithium* sp., a small gastropod which accounted for about 80% of the total sample. The genus *Cerithium* accounted for only 2.01% of the López Viejo shells. In the El Oro sites, 7 species accounted for 98% of all shells, although no single species was an overwhelming dominant except at one site where the mangrove oyster, *Ostrea columbiensis*, constituted 99% of the total.

It is difficult to interpret the great molluscan taxonomic richness and diversity at site OMJPLP15. Only a few species appear to have been routinely employed in the manufacture of shell ornaments (the pearl oysters *P. sterna* and *P. mazatlanica*, the two *Spondylus* species, and *Oliva undatella*) or tools (*Strombus* spp.). While these species may have been collected principally for their ornamental or functional value, presumably their meat was also eaten. The major worked shell species are figured in Appendix B; the drawings have been adapted from Mora Sánchez 1990 (bivalves).

A number of less–common species were apparently sometimes used as ornaments (e.g., *Cypraea* spp. and *Fustiaria splendida*).

Several large species were certainly gathered specifically as food (e.g., *Arca pacifica*, *Raeta undulata*, *Modiolus capax*, *Tivela* sp., and perhaps *Hexaplex* spp. and *Muricanthus* sp.). The chitons and many of the small gastropods (e.g., *Fissurella* spp., *Columbella* spp., *Tegula* spp., *Thais* spp., *Turbo* spp., *Cantharus* spp., and *Olivella semistriata*) presumably also were gathered as food. These species are present in large numbers in all units, were seldom burned, and could not have been collected inadvertently. On the other hand, a few species which live attached to other larger shellfish (e.g., *Serpulorbis* sp., *Crepidula* spp., and *Crucibulum* spp.) were probably collected incidentally with

[1] $H' = - p_i(\ln p_i)$ where p_i is the percentage of taxon i ' n in the sample and n is the total number of taxa identified.

the larger shells.

Some of the less common shell species may have been imported from outside of the immediate region. Among these are *Anadara tuberculosa*, *Chione subrugosa*, and an unidentified pinnid (the only mangrove species found at OMJPLP15), as well as *Malea ringens* (a large gastropod used along the south coast of Ecuador for the manufacture of shell spoons). There remains a large number of uncommon species which may have been collected opportunistically as food along with other more common species or perhaps were collected as curiosities potentially useful in the manufacture of ornaments (e.g., *Trivia* sp., *Astraea* spp., *Simnia aequalis*, *Trophon cerrosensis*, and *Architectonica nobilis*).

Molluscs of López Viejo: Preliminary List

Class / Family / Species	Minimum Number of Individuals
Pelecypoda (bivalves): 64 species	
Anomiidae	
Anomia adamas Gray	4
Anomia peruviana (Orbigny)	1
Arcidae	
Anadara formosa (Orbigny)	3
Anadara nux (Sowerby)	1
Anadara obesa (Sowerby)	9
Anadara tuberculosa (Sowerby)	3
Arca pacifica (Sowerby)	347
Barbatia gradata (Broderip & Sowerby)	2
Barbatia reeveana (Orbigny)	3
Barbatia rostae Berry	1
Litharca lithodomus (Sowerby)	1
Cardiidae	
Trachycardium procerum (Sowerby)	8
Trachycardium senticosum (Sowerby)	11
Trigoniocardia biangulata (Brod. & Sow.)	1
Trigoniocardia guanacastensis (Her. & St.)	10
Carditidae	
Cardita crassicostata (Sowerby)	3
Cardita laticosta Sowerby	1
Cardita radiata Sowerby	1
Chamidae	
Chama sp.	26
Pseudochama sp.	116
Corbiculidae	
Polymesoda inflata (Philippi)	1
Corbulidae	
Corbula ovulata Sowerby	3
Donacidae	
Donax asper Hanley	1
Donax mancorensis Olsson	9
Donax transversus Sowerby	1
Glycymerididae	
Glycymeris delessertii (Reeve)	2
Glycymeris inaequalis (Sowerby)	1
Isognomonidae	
Isognomon janus Carpenter	4

Class Family Species	Minimum Number of Individuals
Mactridae	
Mactra sp. Philippi	1
Mactrellona sp.	3
Raeta undulata (Gould)	125
Mytilidae	
Brachidontes sp.	17
Modiolus capax (Conrad)	102
Nuculanidae	
Nuculana elenensis (Sowerby)	1
Ostreidae	
Ostrea fisheri Dall	1
Ostrea iridescens Hanley	3
Ostrea megodon Hanley	1
Pectinidae	
Argopecten circularis (Sowerby)	2
Lyropecten subnodosus (Sowerby)	24
Pecten sp.	1
Petricolidae	
Petricola denticulata Sowerby	1
Petricola robusta Sowerby	2
Petricola sp. #3	1
Pholadidae	
Jouannetia pectinata (Conrad)	1
Pinnidae	
unidentifiable pinnid #1	12
Plicatulidae	
Plicatula spondylopsis Rochebrune	3
Pteriidae	
Pinctada mazatlanica (Hanley)	174
Pteria sterna (Gould)	751
Semelidae	
Semele sp.	1
Solecurtidae	
Tagelus sp.	9
Spondylidae	
Spondylus calcifer Carpenter	12
Spondylus princeps Broderip	45
Tellinidae	
Strigilla chroma Salisbury	13

Class Family Species	Minimum Number of Individuals
Veneridae	
Chione amathusia (Philippi)	3
Chione mariae (Orbigny)	2
Chione subimbricata (Hanley)	1
Chione subrugosa (Wood)	1
Dosinia dunkeri (Philippi)	3
Megapitaria aurantiaca (Sowerby)	8
Periglypta multicostata (Sowerby)	11
Pitar lupanaria (Lesson)	11
Pitar vinaceus (Olsson)	2
Protothaca beili (Olsson)	1
Protothaca columbiensis (Sowerby)	4
Tivela planulata (Broderip & Sowerby)	1
Gastropoda (snails): 95 species	
Acmaeidae	
Scurria mesoleuca (Menke)	1017
Architectonicidae	
Architectonica nobilis Röding	1
Buccinidae	
Cantharus elegans (Griffith & Pidgeon)	16
Cantharus gemmatus (Reeve)	145
Cantharus ringens (Reeve)	99
Cantharus vibex (Broderip)	4
Bullidae	
Bulla sp.	4
Bursidae	
Bursa caelata (Broderip)	8
Calyptraeidae	
Crepidula aculeata (Gmelin)	28
Crepidula lessonii (Broderip)	3
Crepipatella dorsata (Broderip)	8
Crucibulum scutellatum (Wood)	23
Crucibulum spinosum (Sowerby)	34
Cancellariidae	
Cancellaria urceolata Hinds	1
Cassididae	
Cassis centiquadrata (Valenciennes)	7
Cerithiidae	
Cerithium adustum Kiener	169
Cerithium nicaraguense Pilsbry & Lowe	2

Class Family Species	Minimum Number of Individuals
Columbellidae	
Anachis fluctuata (Sowerby)	5
Columbella fuscata Sowerby	17
Columbella labiosa Sowerby	444
Columbella major Sowerby	424
Columbella strombiformis Lamarck	2
Strombina hirundo (Gaskoin)	1
Strombina recurva (Sowerby)	3
Conidae	
Conus nux Broderip	22
Conus patricius Hinds	1
Conus princeps Linnaeus	44
Cymatiidae	
Cymatium lignarium (Broderip)	1
Cypraeidae	
Cypraea cervinetta Kiener	12
Cypraea sp. # 2	16
Fasciolariidae	
Latirus concentricus (Reeve)	10
Latirus mediamericanus Hertlein & Strong	1
Leucozonia cerata (Wood)	2
Ficidae	
Ficus ventricosa (Sowerby)	12
Fissurellidae	
Fissurella sp. #1	3374
Fissurella sp. #2	51
Fissurella sp. #3	3
Hipponicidae	
Hipponix grayanus Menke	13
Hipponix panamensis C.B. Adams	5
Hipponix pilosus (Deshayes)	28
Littorinidae	
Littorina sp.	36
Melampidae	
Melampus sp.	1
Mitridae	
Mitra tristis Broderip	2
Muricidae	
Eupleura sp.	1
Hexaplex brassica (Lamarck)	13
Hexaplex regius (Swainson)	2
Murexiella sp.	2
Muricanthus sp.	39
Muricopsis zeteki Hertlein & Strong	3
Trophon cerrosensis Dall	2
Vitularia salebrosa (King & Broderip)	2

Class Family Species	Minimum Number of Individuals
Nassariidae	
Nassarius sp.	3
Naticidae	
Natica sp.	1
Polinices panamensis (Récluz)	1
Polinices ravidus (Souleyet)	1
Neritidae	
Nerita funiculata Menke	22
Nerita scabricosta Lamarck	2
Olividae	
Oliva polpasta Duclos	1
Oliva undatella Lamarck	12
Olivella semistriata (Gray)	12064
Ovulidae	
Jenneria pustulata (Lightfoot)	2
Simnia aequalis (Sowerby)	1
Planaxidae	
Planaxis planicostatus Sowerby	135
Potamididae	
Cerithidea mazatlanica Carpenter	1
Siphonariidae	
Siphonaria palmata Carpenter	309
Strombidae	
Strombus gracilior Sowerby	6
Strombus granulatus Swainson	5
Strombus peruvianus Swainson	3
Terebridae	
Hastula luctuosa (Hinds)	2
Thaididae	
Acanthina brevidentata (Wood)	912
Neorapana muricata (Broderip)	16
Purpura pansa Gould	3
Thais biserialis (Blainville)	563
Thais callaoensis (Gray)	1
Thais melones (Duclos)	39
Thais speciosa (Valenciennes)	7
Thais triangularis (Blainville)	64
Tonnidae	
Malea ringens (Swainson)	3
Triviidae	
Trivia radians (Lamarck)	1
Trochidae	
Tegula panamensis (Philippi)	2174
Tegula picta McLean	213

Class
  Family
    Species
	Minimum Number of Individuals

Turbinidae	
Astraea babelis (Fischer)	43
Astraea buschii (Philippi)	13
Turbo magnificus Jonas	58
Turbo saxosus Wood	465
Turbo squamiger Reeve	21
Turritellidae	
Turritella sp.	2
Vasidae	
Vasum caestus (Broderip)	1
Vermetidae	
Serpulorbis sp.	210
Terrestrial Gastropoda	
Strophocheilus sp.	733
Unidentified Gastropoda	
marine sp. #1	575
terrestrial sp. #1	182
terrestrial sp. #2	6
terrestrial sp. #3	1
terrestrial sp. #4	1
Scaphopoda (tusk shells): 1 species	
Dentaliidae	
Fustiaria splendida (Sowerby)	5
Polyplacophora (chitons): 1 species	
chiton sp. #1	1308

Principal Mollusc Species
Employed in the Manufacture of Shell Ornaments

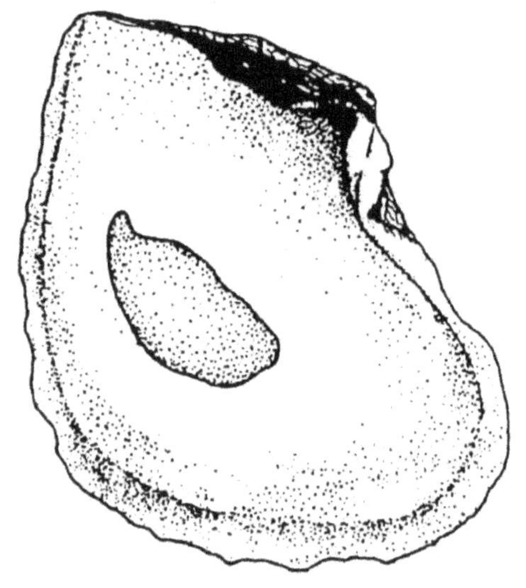

Pinctada mazatlanica

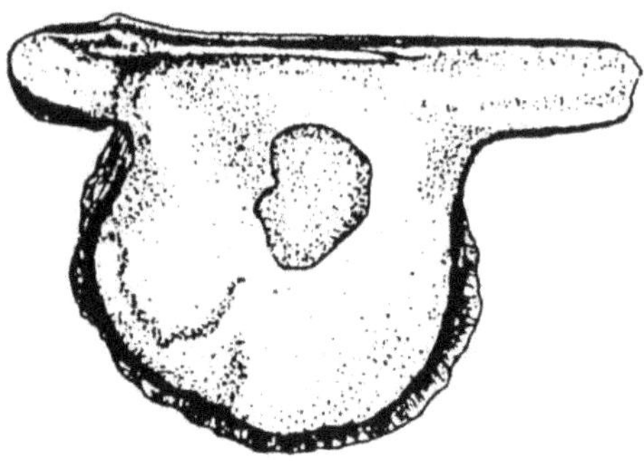

Pteria sterna

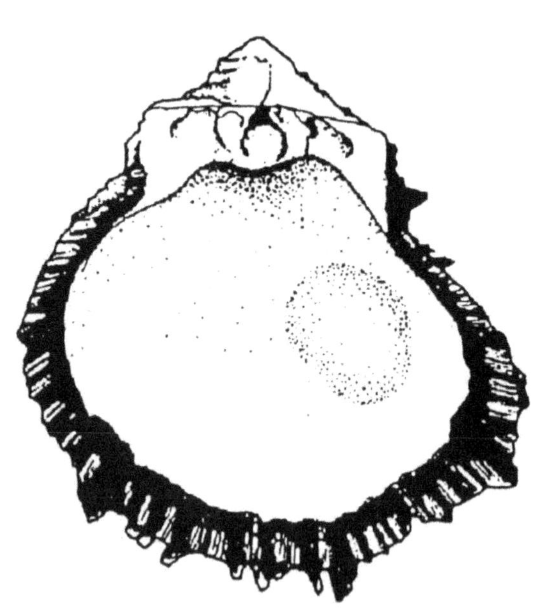

Spondylus princeps

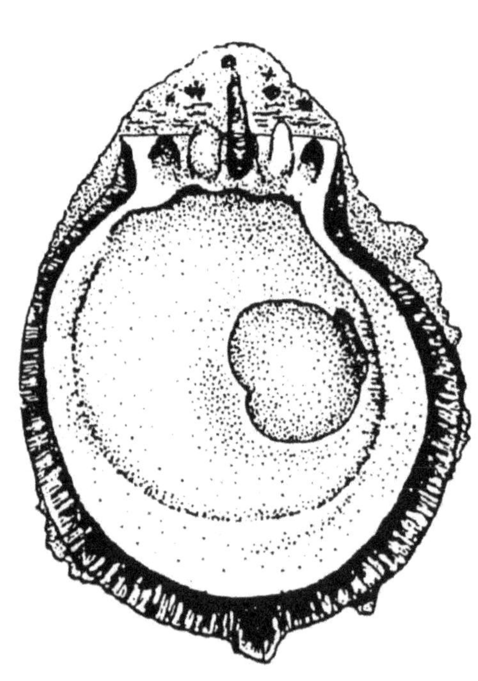

Spondylus calcifer

CHAPTER 5

DISCUSSION

Introduction

Before embarking upon a discussion of the data excavated from the Midden site it is necessary to review briefly the context for specialist shell working and trade on the coast of Ecuador, as there are good ethnohistorical references to both.

Ecuador at European Contact

When Pizarro, leading Spanish expeditionary forces, first arrived off the shores of Ecuador in 1525, they encountered a series of independent established coastal chiefdoms and townships who had not submitted to Inca domination in the way of highland Ecuador. The ethnohistorical record, supported by archaeological data, both attest to the presence of developed, hierarchic societies organised into local or regional chiefdoms, whose economies were centred around the production of textiles, metallurgy and fine pottery. Production was organised within groups of specialist guilds of craftsmen, with different classes of merchant traders (*mindalaes*), seamen, pearl and shell divers and shell craftsmen, whilst the majority of ordinary folk engaged either in fishing or in agriculture (various, e.g. Cieza de Leon, [1532–50] 1864; Meggers, 1966; Norton, 1986, 1992; Oviedo y Valdez, [1550] 1945); Pizarro, [1527] 1844; Pizarro, [1571] 1844; Salomon, 1977/78, 1986). In particular, we know that there were four cities together under one master or lord (Señor), called Calangome (also sp. Calangane), Tusco, Seracapez and Calango which held hegemony over the entire central and north coast of Ecuador (Pizarro [Xerez, 1527] 1844: 199–200).

In the second expedition of Francisco Pizarro in 1525, the author of the *Relación* (probably Francisco de Xerez, secretary to Pizarro) records the capture, by Pizarro's pilot, Bartolomeo Ruiz, of a large, ocean–going balsa raft sailing off the northern Ecuadorean coast. The raft was said to be from a place or town called Calangane (three different spellings are given for this name) and was carrying a large cargo of gold and silver ornaments, richly embroidered textiles, and quantities of the bivalve *Spondylus princeps* (called *mullu*) for which they traded. The extract from his account which follows provides an illuminating description of a prosperous and thriving society at point of European contact.

> ...they took a ship in which came up to twenty men, of which eleven of them threw themselves into the water, and taking three of those left the pilot (Bartolomeo Ruiz) put the others ashore so that they might go; and these three that were kept for interpreters, he treated very well and kept them with him.
>
> This ship which I say he took, seemed to have the capacity of up to thirty *toneles* (about 25 modern tons); it was made in plan and keel of canes as big as posts, bound with ropes of what they call sisal, which is like hemp, and the upper (deck) of lighter canes tied with the same ropes, where the people and their cargo travel together dry because the lower part is awash. Her masts and lateen yards were of very fine wood and sails of cotton of the same appearance as our ships, and very good rigging of the said sisal, which I say is like hemp, and some pierced stone weights (*potales*) for anchors in the manner of barbers' grinding stones.
>
> And they were carrying many items of silver and of gold personal ornament to exchange with those with whom they were going to trade, including crowns and diadems and belts and gauntlets (*ponietes*) and leg armour (greaves?) and breastplates and tweezers and jingling bells and strings and bunches of beads and *rosecleres* (other beads of a clear, rosy colour [Mester, 1990]) and mirrors mounted with the said silver, and cups and other drinking vessels; they carried many mantles of wool and of cotton, and shirts and *aljubas* (tunics?) and *alaremes* (not translated) and many other garments, most of them embroidered and richly worked in colours of scarlet and crimson, and blue and yellow, and of all other colours in different kinds of work and figures of birds and animals and fish and trees; and they brought some tiny weights to weigh gold, like Roman workmanship, and many other things. On some strings of beads there were some small stones of emerald and chalcedony, and other stones and pieces of crystal and *ánime* (not translated). All this they brought to exchange for some shells from which they make coral red and white beads, and they had the vessel almost laden with them.........
>
> Those three indians which I said were seized on the ship (raft) and brought to the captains acquired our language very well. It seems that they were from a land and town called Calangane: the people in that land are of the most superior quality and manner of indians for they are of better appearance and colour and very skilled (wise), and have a dialect like Arabic, and it seems that they had subjection over the indians I spoke of of Tacamez and of the bay of San Mateo, and of Nancabez and of Tovirisimi and Conilope and Papagayos, and Tolona and Quisimos and Coaque and Tonconjes and Arampajaos, and Pintagua and Caraslobez and Amarejos, Cames, Amotopse, Docoa, all towns of the said plain (flat land) that are found along the coast; and of all the rest of the coast in that land of Calangone where they are (come from), there are four towns together, under one master (lord), which are the said Calangome, and Tusco and Seracapez and Calango. There there are many sheep (alpacas) and pigs (wild peccary) and cats (ocelots?) and dogs and other

animals, and geese and pigeons, and there they make the blankets (shawls) that I said above are of wool and of cotton, and the embroidery (needlework) and the beads and items of silver and gold, and it seems are people of much order (good government/civilised): they have many tools of copper and other metals with which they work their lands, and obtain gold and make all manner of profit: their towns have well laid–out streets: they have many kinds of garden produce, and have much order and justice amongst themselves: the women are very fair (beautiful or fair–complexioned) and well–dressed and all for the most part are *labranderas* (probably craft– workers or embroiderers, but possibly also farmers). There is an island in the sea close to the towns where they have a house of prayer made in the manner of a camp tent covered with rich embroidered mantles, where they have an image of a woman with a child in her arms whom they call María Meseia: when someone has an affliction in some part (of the body), they make a copy of the part in silver or in gold, and offer it to her, and they sacrifice sheep (alpacas) before this image at certain times.
(Pizarro [Xerez, 1527], 1844: 196–200; my translation).

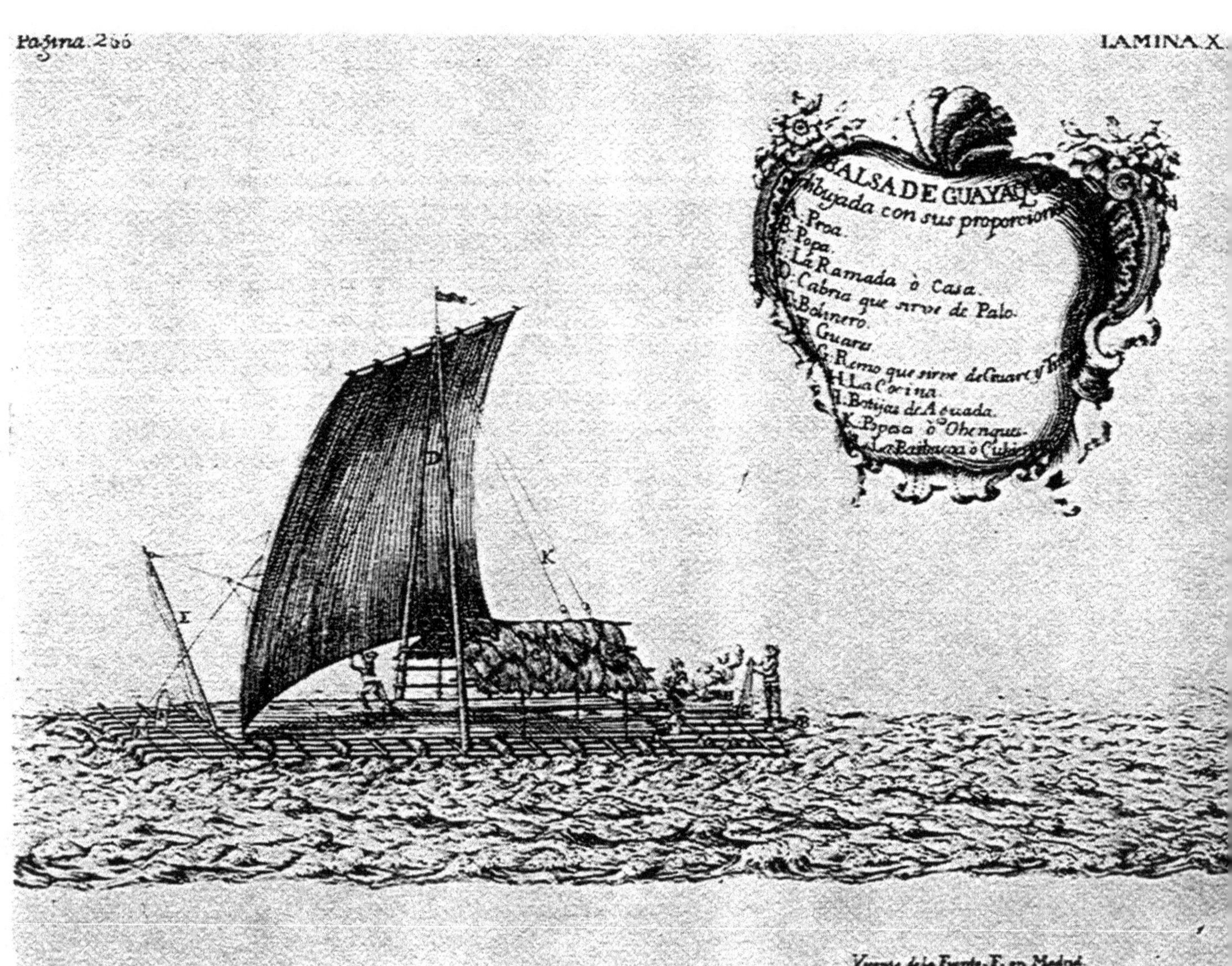

Drawing of an 18th century indigenous *balsa* raft under square sail from Guayaquil, Ecuador (Juan & Ulloa, 1748)

Researchers believe, that the region referred to as Calangome is the same coastal strip containing the modern towns of Machalilla, Agua Blanca, Puerto López and Salango, with the island being that of Isla Salango, situated just offshore in the Bay of Salango. Studies of the relevant ethnohistorical texts (e.g., Silva, 1983) have led to a concensus view that Agua Blanca was Calangome, Machalilla was Tusco, López Viejo Seracapez, with Calango being modern-day Salango (Silva, 1983, cited in Mester, 1990; McEwan, 1994: personal communication). The site of Agua Blanca, located 8 kilometres inland from the coast, almost certainly functioned as the administrative and ceremonial focus for the Manteño, and possibly earlier occupations of this region (McEwan, 1992).

The Shell-Working Industry in Manabí.

Most archaeological sites along the southern Manabí coast have not only abundant surface scatters of pottery, but also marine shells, chert tools, stone net-weights, shell tools, and shell- working debitage indicative of centuries of economic activity focused on the sea. Great concentrations of shell and cut shell may be found along the slopes bordering the southward ends of bays which were, at Contact, heavily populated (Estrada, 1957, 1962; Norton, 1986, 1992; Saville, 1907–1910). Field surveys on the Isla Salango, including those conducted in the early 1980s by members of the Programa de Antropología para el Ecuador, confirm the presence of regular prehistoric use and ceremonial activity from late Valdivia times up to and including the late Manteño period referred to in the above translation (Allan, n.d.; Estrada, 1957b; Norton, 1986; Norton, Lunnis and Nayling, 1984).

Allan (n.d.), reporting on the excavation of a specialist shell workshop at OMJPLP 140, Salango, emphasises the importance of *Spondylus* working there, although the data he presents are difficult to interpret given that we are presented with counts of fragments of shells, rather than weights. However, it seems that *Pinctada mazatlanica* was certainly well-utilised here, whilst the relative paucity of *Spondylus* remains at this site is explained by postulating that it was traded out of the site. Given the demonstrable trade in large quantities of the whole valve southward into Peru, particularly from the Integration period onwards, this may well be true, although strictly speaking it is negative evidence, and the presence of *P.mazatlanica* should not be underestimated in order to exaggerate the value of *Spondylus*.

Artifacts of *Pinctada mazatlanica*, including putative fishhooks and nose-rings, together with *Spondylus* beads, were also recovered during the excavations of Structure 1, OMJPLP 141B (Shotliff, 1987). It is interesting to note that the author does not believe that a shell-working industry was focused at this site, however, as little evidence of debitage or suitable shell- working tools were found here.

Mester (1985, 1990, 1992) presented data on the excavations she carried out at a shell workshop at Los Frailes (Machalilla), a few kilometres to the north of López Viejo, where she was able to establish the importance of both *P. mazatlanica* and *P. sterna* to the long-distance trade networks engaged in along this coast, particularly during the early Manteño period. Interestingly, it seems that the workshops at Los Frailes chiefly utilised *Pteria sterna* for fine items of adornment, rather than *Pinctada mazatlanica*, which was used mainly for utilitarian objects. The inventory of shell artifacts described include plaques, beads, discs, pendants and possible fishhooks. The plaques are described as being rectangular, circular, teardrop and zoomorphic, with one or more holes for suspension and these, for the most part, compare well with the group described in this report, where rectangular plaques: 'blanks', or drilled with two or four holes are also described. Mester's circular plaques would seem to equate to the 'fine' discs group here. The Midden Site also produced zoomorphic shell figures, including those fashioned from *Spondylus* as well as *P. mazatlanica*. Indeed, as we have seen, the majority of the plaques from the Midden Site are fashioned from *P. mazatlanica* rather than *P. sterna* as they were at Los Frailes. Mester also reports finding more than 20 chert drills, which appear to be very similar to those described from the Midden Site, as well as chert and obsidian blades, all presumably used in the shell-working industry at Los Frailes (Mester, 1990: 178).

Excavations at Valdivia sites along the southern Ecuadorean coast: San Pablo, Valdivia itself and San Isidro all contain reports of mother-of-pearl together with *Spondylus*. Meggers, Evans and Estrada illustrate a range of different shell artifacts for both their Valdivia and Machalilla phases, which include very similar discs, centre-cut discs and semi-circular cut discs (which they call fishhooks) to those reported from the Midden Site, López Viejo. Beads and what are called 'fine discs' in this report are also shown (1965: Plates 21, 23, 24, 129, 130).

Pinctada mazatlanica is also reported from archaeological contexts from Isla La Plata, from a Machalilla occupation at the site OM-Pl-Il-12 and from the Chorrera and Bahía levels at OM-Pl- Il-14, where objects interpreted as fishhooks, and deliberately broken fishhooks are described (Marcos and Norton, 1984: 13–14). The evidence of regular ceremonial and trade-orientated activity, often associated with great use of marine shells including *Pinctada* and *Spondylus*, has been demonstrated for Isla La Plata, from the late Valdivia period onwards (Dorsey, 1901; Marcos and Norton, 1981, 1984).

The Importance of Mother-of-Pearl

Much has been made of the key role played by the 'thorny oysters' *Spondylus princeps* and less often *Spondylus calcifer* in the long-distance trading networks developed along the coast of southern Ecuador from at least Valdivia 3 times onwards (Marcos, 1977/8; Marcos and Norton, 1981, 1984; Murra, 1982; Norton, 1986, 1992; Paulsen, 1974; Zeidler, 1991; Zevallos, 1987).

The excavations carried out at the Midden Site OMJPLP15, López Viejo, Puerto López, particularly from the middle and late phases of the Manteño occupation suggest a more important role for the pearl oysters, particularly *P. mazatlanica*, than previously considered. Although artifacts of *Spondylus* do occur, they are principally small beads, whilst artifacts manufactured from *Pinctada* overwhelmingly predominate. In this I entirely concur with Mester, that researchers have continually stressed the importance of *Spondylus* at the expense of species of shell such as the pearl oysters referred to (1990: 19–21). Both ethnohistorical and archaeological data confirm the view that mother–of–pearl, in the form of *Pinctada mazatlanica* and *Pteria sterna*, has been well–utilised throughout prehistory, at least from Valdivia times onwards (e.g., Meggers, Evans and Estrada, 1965; Marcos and Norton, 1984; Mester, 1985, 1990; Topic, 1982; Zevallos and Holm, 1960, in addition to this report).

There are a number of interesting questions raised by these issues. For example, if *Spondylus* were as important as claimed during the Formative periods, does the subsequent rise in the use of the pearl oyster imply a reduction in the quantity of *Spondylus* available locally through the following Regional Developmental and later Integration periods, which may relate to its increasing importance as a valuable commodity of long– distance trade? It may also be true that the importance of the pearl oyster fisheries during the earlier periods of prehistory has always been underestimated.

A Diversity of Production at López Viejo

The cumulative data from the excavations at López Viejo, support the view that the Midden site was located close to or within the site of an ancient production area for decorative ornaments. Moreover, the range of special artifacts, for example, the large numbers of chert tools, the copper needles, pins, and other tools, the bone pins, and the array of decorative ornamental goods: shell beads of several types, shell figures, crescents, copper bells and rings, hollow bone segments and ceramic tubular beads, all point to the production of finished goods here, whether items of jewellery, such as necklaces, collars, headdresses and bracelets, or decorated clothing. The presence of spindle whorls further suggests the manufacture of twine for the weaving of cloth on–site, or at least for the production of thread with which to string together finished necklaces or for sewing ornaments to clothing. Ethnohistoric records (e.g., Cieza de Leon, 1864; Oviedo y Valdés, 1945) document the Manteño as producing fine woven cotton textiles for trade, a fact further supported by the description of the goods from the captured trading raft.

Readers will note the close parallel between details of the range of artifacts discovered during the course of the excavations, and the goods referred to in the text quoted above as being carried on the trading raft. Of particular note are the copper goods, including tweezers and bells, the strings and bunches of red and white shell beads and the richly decorated garments. There is either direct or indirect evidence for these goods from the excavations at López Viejo.

It is interesting to consider the lack of specialisation manifest here, however. Chert drills and obsidian knives for working the shell were evidently produced on site, given the large quantities of debitage and by the finding of flaking tools, such as the cut deer antler and, most probably, the *Strombus* (?) shell points. Small quantities of slag, perhaps from copper smelting are also possible (subject to laboratory confirmation). It should be borne in mind that copper is not native to the area, and it seems likely that the most convenient sources were from northern Peru, with whom the Manteño were evidently trading *Spondylus* and other goods.

The whole question of the use of copper axe 'money', or *moneda hacha* (*naipes* from northern Peru), has been addressed by a number of researchers (e.g., Holm, 1966–7; Hosler, 1988a, 1988b; Hosler *et al* 1990; Meggers, 1966; Shimada, 1985, 1990; Zevallos, 1987), where it is suggested that I and T shaped flat copper ingots were used as a standard of exchange. None have been recovered from López Viejo, but the presence of copper artifacts is, in itself, evidence of such exchange. The range of copper special artifacts found: rings, needles, pins, fishhooks, bells and tweezers, as well as paralleling the description of goods found aboard the trading raft, are common to the inventory of Northern Andean copper artifacts in general (e.g., Muse, 1991), which were traded as far as the west coast of Central America, whence metallurgy was first introduced, possibly by Manteño merchants from the Manabí coast around AD 800 (Hosler, 1988a; West, 1961; Zevallos, 1987).

To complete the picture of diversity of production, we have the evidence from the shell identifications and analysis presented in this report of great shellfish species diversity. Although certain shell species were undoubtedly favoured, for example the mother–of–pearl oyster *Pinctada mazatlanica*, less commonly *Pteria sterna*, *Spondylus princeps* and *Spondylus calcifer*, and the cylindrical *Oliva undatella*, very many other species of shell were brought up to the site, and it is unlikely that all these were purely for food consumption, as many have little food value, and, moreover, do not show any evidence of the breakage patterns typical of meat extraction.

Nature of Settlement at the Midden Site

At present it is not possible to reconstruct the character of the settlement in the locality of the Midden site, except to confirm that the mound of occupation debris was situated close to a structure on its eastern side, part of which spreads into the trench in the form of the artificial mound of yellow clay and gravel. Possibly there may have been a number of smaller structures or working areas surrounding this locality where different items were produced, all working towards the goal of a range of finished goods for local consumption or for trade. It is also possible that one large single workshop produced all the goods found. It is hoped to be able to answer these important questions on the nature and organisation of craftsmanship in López Viejo with future research. The implied lack of specialisation here is particularly interesting in the light of ethnohistoric reports from the north coast of Peru, which confirm the very strict implementation of craft specialism there (Rostworowski,

1977). Mester similarly interprets her data as indicating a high degree of craft specialism at the Los Frailes shell workshop (Mester, 1990), but I would argue that for the occupation and industry represented at the Midden Site, the opposite seems more likely to have been the case.

One important outstanding question is the nature of the burial contents of the bell–shaped shaft grave, which, owing to a lack of time for its scientific excavation at the end of the 1993 field season, was left unopened for a future season. Clearly of the early Manteño period, its presence here is enigmatic. It has been suggested that the Manteño never located their elite buials within the confines of their settlements (Presley Norton, 1993: personal communication), although such burials are nevertheless sometimes found there. For example, Mester found a bell–shaped shaft grave at Los Frailes workshop. Although the grave goods did not suggest a particularly elite burial, there is the possibility that it may have been secondary or robbed (Mester, 1990: 140). Meggers (1966: 125) reports that the relative rarity of shaft tombs suggests their construction for individuals of high rank (see also Cieza de Leon (1866: 188). This was certainly the case with the elite burials from Batan Grande, far north coast Peru of the Middle Sicán period (Shimada, 1985, 1990).

Drawing of an indigenous *balsa* raft with original–style lateen sails from Paita Harbour, north coast of Peru, 1614–18 (Spillbergen, 1619)

CHAPTER 6

CONCLUSION

Our work at López Viejo, centered upon a production area for luxury ornaments that in all likelihood contributed to the long–distance trade referred to above, directs our attention to the pivotal role played by the sea–faring Manteño league of merchants (Jijón y Caamaño, 1930) in their wide–ranging contacts with kingdoms as far apart as Mexico and Peru, operating from settlements such as this.

Sicán lords on the Peruvian north coast, and the Chimu kings who succeeded them, purportedly walked upon powdered seashell dust, scattered before them (Conrad, 1982; Cordy–Collins, 1990; Rowe, 1948: 47). There is a long history of veneration of *Spondylus* throughout Peru from the late Preceramic period where it occurs at sites such as Paloma, Aspero and La Galgada, increasing with time through the Early Horizon when it it found represented on the Supreme Deity at Chavín de Huantar, into Early Intermediate Mochica sites in the Moche valley such as Pampa Grande. Eventually, huge quantities of the shell, whole, worked, powdered and burned are found in the rich burial contexts from Late Intermediate sites from the valleys of the La Leche, Lambayeque and Moche rivers, with the rise of the Sicán polities around AD 750 and later with their conquest by Chimor, dating from around ca AD 1350 onwards (Conrad, 1982; Richardson *et al*, 1990; Rowe, 1967; Shimada, 1985, 1990; Topic, 1982).

We know that Peruvian myth and ritual involved intensive consumption of both *Spondylus* and also use of the conch shell *Strombus* (Burger, 1992; Cordy–Collins, 1990; Davidson, 1982), both of which naturally occur only as far south as the Gulf of Guayaquil in Ecuador (Keen, 1971). *Pinctada mazatlanica* and *Pteria sterna*, which have a similar warm water distributional range as *Spondylus* and *Strombus*, have apparently also played an important role in the long–distance trade in coveted tropical sea shells. In this it would seem that, whether *Spondylus*, *Pteria* or *Pinctada*, the ancient Ecuadoreans had managed to foster a demand which only they could supply.

There has not been the scope here to do more than touch upon many issues. It is nevertheless interesting to see history and archaeology complementing one another, and giving us two viewpoints of this undeniably important era of precolumbian merchant adventurers and their trade.

This is the First Report on the Excavations at the Midden Site, OMJPLP15, López Viejo, Puerto López, Manabí, Ecuador. It does not set out to be a comprehensive presentation, analysis and interpretation of all excavated data, but aims to present details of the excavations, together with a description of the special artifacts and a broad overview of finds, to offer a preliminary interpretation on the Midden site, its occupation and its role in the overall context of the prehistory of this part of the coast.

Results of the excavations and the analysis of more than 2000 special artifacts to date suggest that much new and important data will be obtained on the nature of the prehistoric occupation of this interesting area, and in particular, of the shell– working, copper and lithics industries here. It is also expected to be able to develop a new or an amended ceramic sequence for the area, based upon the stratigraphic excavations described above. This will be tested against the existing typologies and sequence of phases, and where inconsistencies emerge, these will be highlighted for further investigation.

I am pleased to report the successful conclusion of Phases 1 and 2 of the project entitled "Prehistory of the Southern Manabí Coast, Ecuador", and to confirm that further levels of data analysis are to be carried out in 1994. These will include a detailed study of the pottery, together with a report on the excavations undertaken at Trench B of The Midden Site. These will be included in the planned Second Report on the Excavations at the Midden Site, López Viejo, Manabí.

REFERENCES

Allan, R. n.d. Site OMJPLP140 A Specialist Shell Workshop. unpublished report, Programa de Antropología para el Ecuador, Salango, Manabí, Ecuador.

Burger, R. L. 1992. *Chavin and the Origins of Andean Civilisation.* Thames and Hudson, London.

Cieza de León, P. 1864. *The Travels of Pedro de Cieza de Leon, AD 1532–50, contained in the First Part of his Chronicle of Peru.* First Series, Volume 33. Translated and edited by Clements R. Markham. Hakluyt Society Edition. London .

Clark, K. E. and P. Netherly. 1990. Las Colecciones de Concha del Proyecto Arqueológico Tahuín y su Significancia para Entender Sistemas de Subsistencia en el Pasado: Informe Preliminar. unpub. report, Proyecto Arqueológico Tahuín, Museo del Banco Central de Ecuador, Guayaquil.

Conrad, G. W. 1982. The Burial Platforms of Chan Chan: Some Social and Political Implications. In M. E. Moseley and K. C. Day (editors) *Chan Chan: Andean Desert City.* A School of American Research Book, University of New Mexico Press, Alburqurque: 87–117.

Cordy–Collins, A. 1990. Fonga Sidge, Shell Purveyor to the Chimu Kings. In M. E. Moseley and A. Cordy–Collins (editors) *The Northern Dynasties: Kingship and Statecraft in Chimor.* A Symposium at Dumbarton Oaks 12th and 13th October 1985. Dunbarton Oaks Research Library and Collection. Washington, D.C: 393–417.

Davidson, J. 1982. Ecology, Art, and Myth: A Natural Approach to Symbolism. In A. Cordy–Collins (editor) *Pre–Columbian Art History: Selected Readings.* Peek Publications, Palo Alto, California: 331–343.

Dorsey, G. A. 1901. Archaeological Investigations on the Island of La Plata, Ecuador. *Field Museum of Natural History Publication* 56, Chicago.

Estrada, E. 1957. *Los Huancavilcas. Ultimas Civilizaciones Pre–Históricas de la Costa del Guayas.* Publicacion del Museo Víctor Emilio Estrada No. 3.

1962. *Arqueología de Manabí Central.* Publicación del Museo Victor Emilio Estrada. No. 7.

Harris, E. 1989. *The Principles of Archaeological Stratigraphy.* Second Edition, London, Academic Press.

Holm, O. 1966–67. Money Axes from Ecuador. *Folk,* Volume 8–9: 135–143.

Hosler, D. 1988a. Ancient West Mexican Metallurgy: South and Central American Origins and West Mexican Transformations. *American Anthropologist* 90 (4): 832–855.

Hosler, D. 1988b. The Metallurgy of Ancient West Mexico. In R. Maddin (editor) *The Beginning of the Use of Metals and Alloys, Zhengzhou, China, 21–26 October, 1986.* Cambridge, MA: MIT Press: 328–343.

Hosler, D., H. Lechtman and O. Holm. 1990. Axe–monies and Their Relatives. *Studies in Pre–Columbian Art and Archaeology.* No. 30. Dunbarton Oaks Research Library and Collections. Washington, D.C.

Jijon y Caamaño, J. 1930. Una Gran Marea Cultural en el Noroeste de Sud América. *Journal de la Societé des Americanistes de Paris* 22, Paris (cited in Mester, 1990; Norton, 1986 and others).

Juan & Ulloa. 1748. *Relación histórica del viaje a la América Meridional* – 4 vols. Madrid.

Keen, A. M. 1971. *Sea Shells of Tropical West America. Marine Mollusks from Baja California to Peru.* 2nd Edition. Stanford University Press, Stanford, California.

Lathrap, D. W. 1975. *Ancient Ecuador. Culture, Clay and Creativity 3000–300 B.C.* Field Museum of Natural History, Chicago, Illinois.

Marcos, J. G. 1977/78. Cruising to Acapulco and Back with the Thorny Oyster Set: A Model for a Lineal Exchange System. *Journal of the Steward Anthropological Society* 9 (1–2): 99–132.

Marcos, J. G. and P. Norton. 1981. Interpretación sobre la Arqueología de la Isla de la Plata. *Miscelánia Antropológica Ecuatoriana.* Boletín de los Museos del Banco Central del Ecuador, Guayaquil. Volume 1: 136–154.

1984. From the *Yungas* of Chinchay Suvo to Cuzco: the Role of La Plata Island in the *Spondylus* Trade. In: D.L. Browman, R.L. Burger and M.A. Rivera (editors) *Social and Economic Organisation in the Prehispanic Andes. Proceedings of the 44th International Congress of Americanists, Manchester, 1982.* BAR International Series 194: 7–21.

McEwan, C. 1992. Sillas de Poder. In Presley Norton and Marco Vincio García (editors) *5000 Años del Ocupacion.* Parque Nacional Machalilla: 53–70.

Meggers, B. J. 1966. *Ecuador.* Ancient Peoples and Places. Thames and Hudson, London.

Meggers, B. J. C. Evans and E. Estrada. 1965. Early Formative Period of Coastal Ecuador: The Valdivia and Machalilla Phases. *Smithsonian Contributions to Anthropology* Volume 1. Smithsonian Institution, Washington.

Mester, A. M. 1985. Un Taller Manteño de Concha Madre Perla del Sitio Los Frailes, Manabí. *Miscelanea Antropologica Ecuatoriana.* Boletín de los Museos del Banco Central del Ecuador, Guayaquil. Volume 5: 101–112.

1990. The Pearl Divers of Los Frailes: Archaeological and Ethnohistorical Explorations of Sumptuary Good Trade and Cosmology in the North and Central Andes. unpub. Ph.D. Dissertation, University of Illinois, Urbana–Champaign.

1992. Un Taller Manteño de la Concha Madre Perla. In Presley Norton and Marco Vincio García (editors) *5000 Años del Ocupacion*, Parque Nacional Machalilla: 41–52.

Mora Sánchez, E. 1990. Catálogo de Bivalvos Marinos del Ecuador. Instituto Nacional de Pesca. *Boletín Científico y Técnico* 10 (1). Guayaquil.

Muse, M. 1991. Products and Politics of a Milagro Entrepôt: Peñón del Río, Guayas Basin, Ecuador. *Research in Economic Anthropology*, 13: 269–323. JAI Press Inc.

Murra, J. V. 1982. El tráfico del *mullu* en la costa del Pacífico. *Primer Simposio de Correlaciones Antropológicas Andino– Mesoamericanos. July 25–31, 1971. Salinas, Ecuador*. J.G. Marcos and P. Norton (editors). Guayaquil, Escuela Superior Politécnica del Litoral: 265–274.

Norton, P. 1986. El Señorio de Salangone y la Liga de Mercadores. El cartel Spondylus–Balsa. *Miscelanea Antropologica Ecuatoriana* Boletín de los Museos del Banco Central del Ecuador, Guayaquil. Volume 6: 131–144.

1992. Los Argonautas del Pacífico Oriental. In Presley Norton and Marco Vincio García (editors) *5000 Años del Ocupacion*. Parque Nacional Machalilla: 1–8.

Olsson, A. A. 1961. *Mollusks of the Tropical Eastern Pacific. Particularly from the Southern Half of the Panamic–Pacific Faunal Province (Panama to Peru). Panamic–Pacific Pelecypoda*. Paleontological Research Institution, Ithaca, New York.

Oviedo y Valdes, G. F de. 1945. *Historia General y Natural de las Indias Islas y Tierra– Firme del Mar Oceano* (ca. 1550). Asunción: Editorial Guarania, Tomo XI.

Paulsen, A.C. 1974. The Thorny Oyster and the Voice of God: *Spondylus* and *Strombus* in Andean Prehistory. *American Antiquity* 39 (4): 597–607.

Pizarro, F. [1527] 1844. Relación de los Primeros Descubrimientos de Francisco Pizarro y Diego de Almagro. In M. Fernandez Navarrete, M. Salvá and P. Sainz de Baranda (editors) *Coleccion de Documentos Inéditos para la Historia de España*, 5: 193–201. Madrid. N.B. (Other authors cite Sámano–Xeréz, J. It seems likely this *Relación* was written by Francisco de Xerez, Pizarro's secretary, then forwarded to Emperor Charles V by Juan de Sámano).

Pizarro, P. [1571] 1844. Relacion del Descubrimiento y Conquista de los Reinos del Peru. In M. Fernandez Navarrete, M. Salvá and P. Sainz de Baranda (editors) *Coleccion de Documentos inéditos para la Historia de España*, 5: 201–388. Madrid.

Richardson, J. B. III., M. A. McConaughy, A. Heaps de Peña and E. B. Décima Zamecnik. 1990. The Northern Frontier of the Kingdom of Chimor: The Piura, Chira, and Tumbez Valleys. In M. E. Moseley and A. Cordy– Collins (editors) *The Northern Dynasties Kingship and Statecraft in Chimor*. A Symposium at Dumbarton Oaks 12th and 13th October 1985. Dunbarton Oaks Research Library and Collection. Washington, D.C: 419–445.

Rostworowski, M. de Diez Canseco. 1977. Coastal Fishermen, Merchants, and Artisans in Pre-Hispanic Peru. In E. P. Benson (editor) *The Sea in the Pre–Columbian World*. A Conference at Dunbarton Oaks, October 26th and 27th, 1974. Dunbarton Oaks Research Library and Collections. Washington, D.C: 167–188.

Rowe, J. H. 1948. The Kingdom of Chimor. *Acta Americana*. Review of the Interamerican Society of Anthropology and Geography. 6 (1): 26–59.

1967. Form and Meaning in Chavin Art. In J.H. Row and D. Menzel (editors) *Peruvian Archaeology: Selected Readings*. Peek Publications, Palo Alto, California: 72–103.

Salomon, F. 1977/78. Pochteca and Mindalá: A Comparison of Long–Distannce Traders in Ecuador and Mesoamerica. *Journal of the Steward Anthropological Society*, 9 (1&2): 231–248.

1986. *Native Lords of Quito in the Age of the Incas. The political economy of north Andean chiefdoms*. Cambridge University Press.

Saville, M. H. 1907–1910. The Antiquities of Manabí, Ecuador. *Contributions to South American Archaeology, Heye Expedition*. 2 volumes. The George G. Heye Foundation, New York.

Shimada, I. 1985. Perception, Procurement, and Management of Resources: Archaeological Perspective. In S. Masuda, I. Shimada and C. Morris (editors) *Andean Ecology and Civilization*. Papers from Wenner–Gren Foundation for Anthropological Research Symposium No. 91. University of Tokyo Press: 357–399.

1990. Cultural Continuities and Discontinuities on the Northern Coast of Peru, Middle–Late Horizons. In M. E. Moseley and A. Cordy–Collins (editors) *The Northern Dynasties Kingship and Statecraft in Chimor*. A Symposium at Dumbarton Oaks 12th and 13th October 1985. Dunbarton Oaks Research Library and Collection. Washington, D.C: 297–392.

Shotliff, A. 1987.Worked Shell from Structure I, OMJPLP 141B. Unpublished Report.

Silva, M. I. 1983. Toponymic Reconstruction as a Basis for Analyzing Social, Economic, and Political Relationships Among Contact Period Settlements on the Central Coast of Ecuador. Paper presented at the 11th Annual Midwest Andean and Amazonian Archaeology and Ethnohistory Conference, Bloomington, Indiana, February, 1983 (cited in Mester, 1990).

Spence, C. (editor). 1990. *Archaeological Site Manual*. Department of Urban Archaeology, Museum of London. Second Edition.

Spillbergen, J. Van. 1619. *Speculum Orientalis Occidentalis que Indiae navigation* 1614–18. Leiden.

Topic, T. Lange. 1982. The Early Intermediate period and its Legacy. In M. E. Moseley and K. C. Day (editors) *Chan Chan: Andean Desert City*. A School of American Research Book, University of New Mexico Press, Alburqurque: 255–284.

West, R. C. 1961. Aboriginal Sea navigation between Middle and South America. *American*

Anthropologist 63 (1): 133–135.

Zeidler, J. A. 1991. Maritime Exchange in the Early Formative Period of Coastal Ecuador: Geopolitical Origins of Uneven Development. In *Research in Economic Anthropology* Volume 13: 247–268. JAI Press Inc.

Zevallos–Menendez, C. 1987. *La Gran Navegacion Prehispanica en el Ecuador*. Coleccion Doctor Honoris Causa – Universidad de Guayaquil No. 2.

Zevallos–Menedez, C. and O. Holm. 1960. Los Anzuelos de Concha y su Valor como Elemento Diagnóstico en las Culturas Ecuarorianas. *Akten des 34 Internationalen Amerikanistenkongresses*. Vienna (cited in Mester, 1990).404– 410.

P. mazatlanica discs

P. mazatlanica semi–circular cut discs and pendant ornament

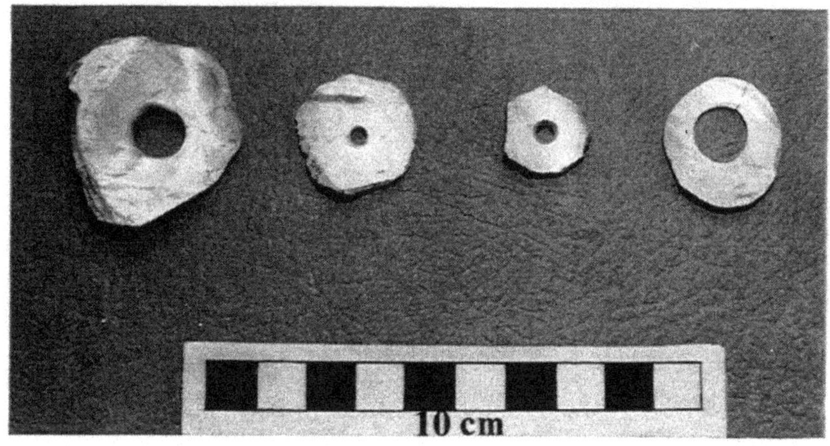

P. mazatlanica centre–cut discs

P. mazatlanica and *P. sterna* rectangular plaques in different stages of work

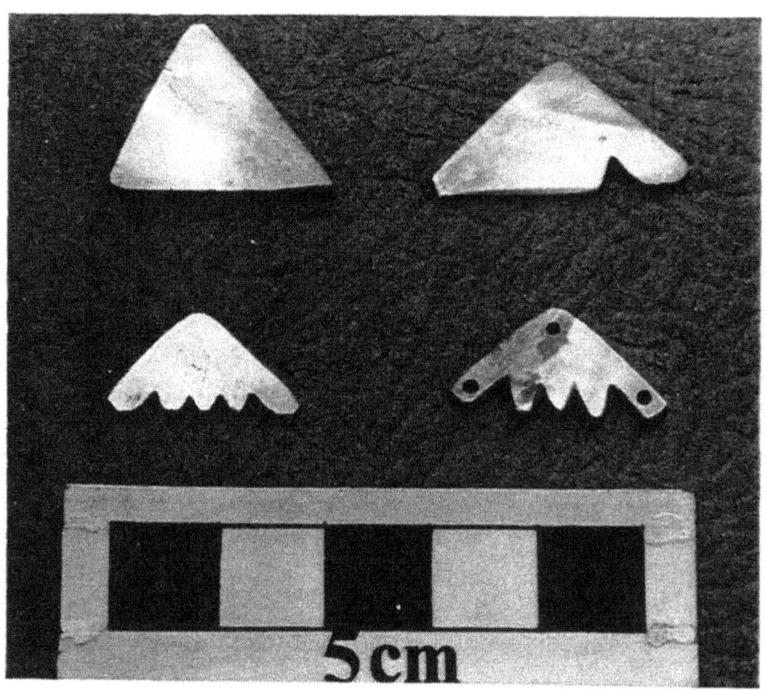

P. mazatlanica triangles in different stages of work

P. mazatlanica crescents

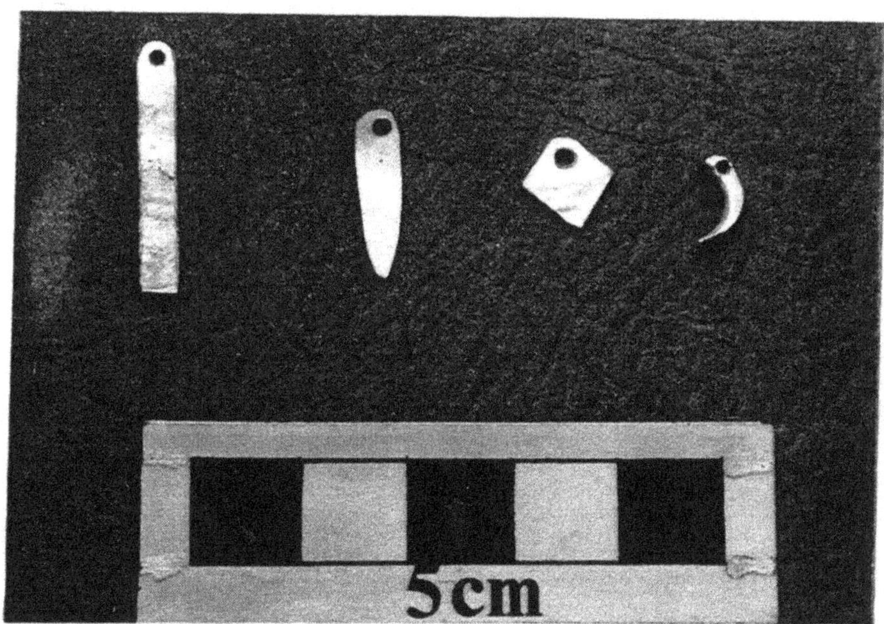

P. mazatlanica ornaments

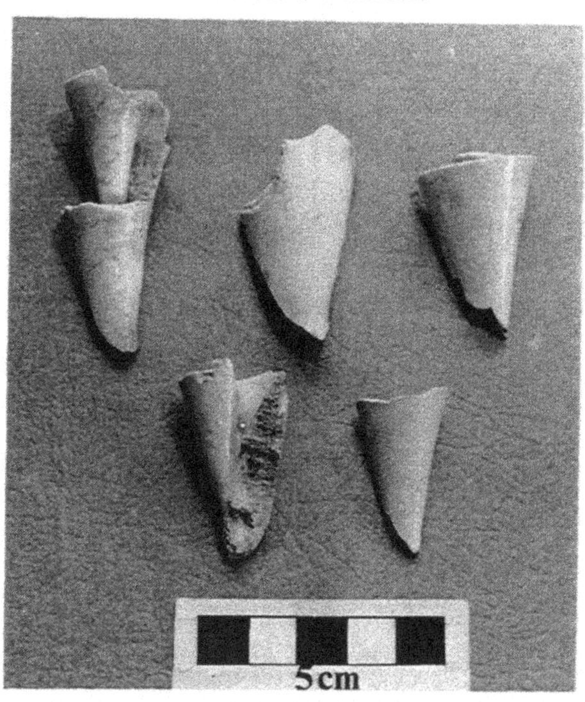

Strombus shell tools

Ceramic grooved tubular beads

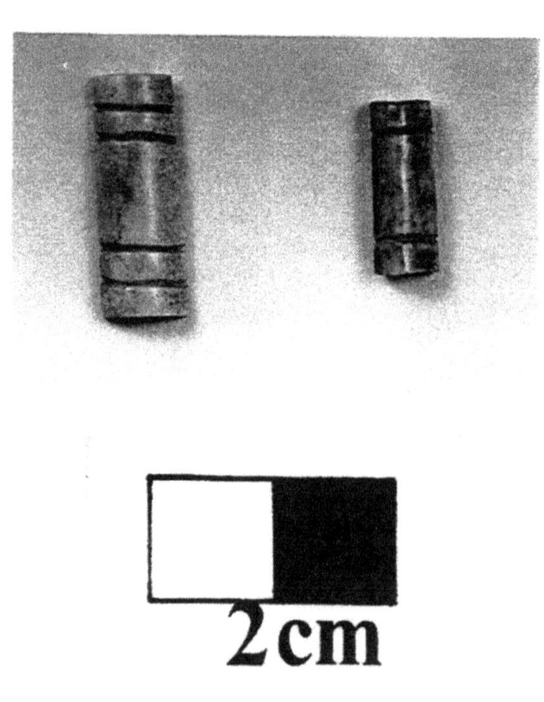

Bone segments

Polished stone weight

P. mazatlanica and *Spondylus* bored figures

P. mazatlanica bored figures

Manteño polished redware jar

Ceramic discs

www.ingramcontent.com/pod-product-compliance
Lightning Source LLC
Chambersburg PA
CBHW051309270326
41929CB00029B/3469